BORTH:
A MARITIME HISTORY

Borth:
a maritime history

Terry Davies

First published in 2009

© Terry Davies/Gwasg Carreg Gwalch

© Llygad Gwalch 2009

Cover design: Sian Parri

Published by Llygad Gwalch,
12 Iard yr Orsaf, Llanrwst, Wales LL26 0EH
tel: 01492 624031
fax: 01492 641502
email: books@carreg-gwalch.com
internet: www.carreg-gwalch.com

*As in the previous book, this work is dedicated
to the beloved memory of my grandmother Mary Davies,
and to Ted and Pam Richards, who made it all possible;*

*to the people of Borth and its environs,
who gave support succour and love in the days of my youth;*

*and to the wonderful unforgettable characters now gone,
save in my dreams,
who were, and are, part of the rich fabric of my experience.*

Er cof am hen bobl y Borth gynt ... halen daear a môr Cymru.

*Inman Cottage, Borth, circa 1900, home of the Lloyd family at some time
during the eighteenth and nineteenth centuries*

ACKNOWLEDGEMENTS

I wish to acknowledge with gratitude, the support and assistance of many people who have helped in my research for this book.

Those whom I interviewed I thank for their patience and generosity, as it has been a pleasure to record their stories – a valuable contribution to the maritime history of Borth, and thereby of Wales. I am indebted to those who allowed me to publish their private photographs and ships' paintings, most of which have hitherto not been seen publicly.

I am grateful also to those who provided family histories based on their private researches. There is no bibliography or reference section in this book, as it is from private data collected over the years that has already been acknowledged in the previous book, *Borth: a Seaborn Village*. One invaluable reference source that I use continually is Dr Reg. Davies' *Welsh Mariners' Index*.

Finally, my thanks to my partner Amanda Shaw, who has been indispensable to this project as a peerless researcher, typist, computer whiz and photographer.

Contents

Introduction

Borth's history reveals a resourceful people living in unimaginable poverty in tiny crowded cottages, built precariously on an exposed coastal shingle bank, flanked on one side by a gale lashed storm beach, and on the other the marshland of Cors Fochno. The villagers existed on fish, milk and bread. Contact with the outside world came once a week in the form of the *Shipping Gazette*, which was bought across the estuary from Aberdyfi by boat. Despite all this, they managed to prosper. Through intelligence, a fiercely independent spirit and astounding courage, they succeeded in a hostile environment. They were outward-looking and sailed the worlds' oceans to far-flung ports and cities, which they often knew better than the conurbations of their own hinterland. For example, Captain William Hughes (b. 1842), sailed the brig *Fanny Fothergill* to trade in Australian waters in the 1870s. Hugh James (b. 1844) sailed the barques *Hawarden Castle* and the *Carmarthen Castle* around the world to ports on the west coast of America, the Orient and South Africa. Captain Lewis Williams voyaged round Cape Horn a dozen times on his way to Wellington, New Zealand and Melbourne, Australia. Captain T. C. Enos knew the ports of the east and west coasts of America like the back of his hand, especially those of Peru and Chile, as he had spent years in the Peruvian Navy. Captain John Williams (b. 1836) sailed the small 588 ton barque *Glendovey*, owned by fellow-villager William James, all over the world for forty years up to 1900.

Borth seafarers are mentioned in a 1678 survey of fishermen and mariners; there were fourteen from the Borth area. Llandre churchyard reveals that many villagers were seafarers in the 1700s, such as Captain Richard Jones, who ran the sloop *Britannia* in the 1750s. Captain Thomas Thomas (b. 1793) captained the Caernarfon brig *Elizabeth* at twenty-six years old. Thomas Hughes (1721–78) and Hugh Richards (1733–1800), are noted as mariners on their gravestones. There were master mariners Enoch James (b. 1779) and William Thomas (b. 1770). Local sloop captains John Jones, John Rees, John Thomas, David Daniel, David Hughes, David Morgan, Hugh Humphreys and Thomas Daniel, all sailed in the 1700s.

For centuries, Borth was dependent on herring. Its first mention is to do with the tithes being extracted from boats moored at Borth and Aberleri in 1373 AD. In Elizabethan times it was mentioned as a gathering site for seasonal fishing craft. In 1898, in an October edition of the *Cambrian News*, it was reported that Borth people would have to suffer a dire winter because of the lack of herrings in the bay. Children often went with the grown-ups to chase the seasonal harvest and learned their seamanship at an early age, in what could often prove treacherous conditions. Boat-launching from a storm beach is not for the faint-hearted; nor is returning. In 1810 one of Captain Davies Maesteg's antecedents drowned with other Borth men whilst returning from herring fishing. Even the most experienced boatmen can succumb to accidents. During a stormy November in 1871, there was a near disaster as ten Borth boats were caught in a storm. Although some landed safely, three were swamped, and a crewmember of the *Mary Ann* nearly drowned as he became entangled in nets under the overturned boat.

Borth mariners were proud of their achievements, and especially of the ships they served on or owned: to such a degree that they named their houses after them; a few of these are Gleanor, Leander, Hopewell, Ivanhoe, Sabrina, Emmett, Convoy, Mayfield and Acorn. The schooner *Acorn* which sailed for over eighty years, was captained and owned by John Rees (b. 1820). This vessel sailed under his command from 1864 to 1880, back and forth to the Mediterranean. Sadly, her end came when she was eventually sunk by a U-boat in 1917. Her name lived on at Acorn House, later Mr. Budge's Acorn Garage, and nowadays, the Acorn Fish and Chip Shop. The house name Munding came from the SS *Godmunding*, captained by Thomas Jones (1845–96).

The offspring of those who settled in the village to work with the railways, the lead mining industry or as canal cutters redirecting the Leri into the Dyfi also became gripped by 'sea fever'. Richard Collins (1791–1818) was a mariner who died at twenty-seven years old, and is buried in Llandre churchyard. John George served for years on the Aberdyfi built brigantine the *Xanthus*. The two seafaring Pierce brothers, John and Thomas, served on the schooner *Lorne*. Arthur Lunt (b. 1848) was bosun on the schooner *Cambrian* in the 1870s. John Hughes Oddy, son of local butcher Thomas Oddy, passed as captain in November 1885. Thomas Bywater (1870–95) began his career as ship's boy on the schooner *Cambrian* and later mate on the *Carnegie*; his brother William (1865–1907) was captain of the *Gatesgarth* in 1891. John Bracegirdle, who lived at Frondirion, retired in 1914 after serving sixteen years in the Royal Navy.

The Tibbot brothers, Thomas and John, both served in the RNR in World War One, John on the *HMS Tiger*, and afterwards, for a time, in the Merchant Navy. Thomas Hughes Dutton (1865–1915) was the son of George Dutton, a platelayer from Chester, who settled in Borth and married a local Hughes girl. As a young man Thomas served on the last of the fabled Swansea copper ore ships, rounding Cape Horn several times. By the age of twenty-seven he was a master mariner and worked for a shipping company based in the Orient, and often met up with two other Borth men, Captain Davies of Maesteg and Captain Thomas of London House, in Shanghai. Captain Dutton died in 1915 at Sapele, West Africa, whilst commander of the Elder Dempster liner *Patania*.

John Taylor (b. 1876) became captain in 1912. His family had been in Borth since the 1790s, and his grandfather John was a veteran of the Battle of Waterloo. George William Meddins became chief engineer in 1916. John Ivor Kinsey (1907–40), the son of David Thomas and Margretta Kinsey, was a radio officer in the Merchant Navy, but lost his life in 1940 when the *SS Dalblair* of Newcastle on Tyne was sunk by enemy action. Captain Elie Robilliard came to Borth with his wife Vera, in 1920. He was of French extraction and had married a Welsh girl from Barry with connections to Borth. His family had lived since the 1700s on Guernsey in the Channel Islands, most of the males becoming either farmers or mariners. Eli and Vera's first child, a girl called Betty, died in 1927 at six years old. They subsequently had two sons, David (b. 1930) and John (b. 1939). Captain Robilliard was lost whilst in command of the *SS Creekirk* of London when she was torpedoed in 1940. His elder son David attended Towyn School after leaving Upper Borth Primary School. He was at sea for a decade and became third mate serving on the *Hoperidge* and the *Rumney*, often voyaging to Australia. He joined Trinity House and served for a year on the *South Goodwin Lightship*. Torteval, the Robilliard ancestral home in the Channel Islands, gave its name to the house in Upper Borth.

Other seafarers have come to live in the village. Harold Austin 'Sammy' Samson, a Merchant Navy man, arrived to work on the sea defences some sixty years ago. His son David has been a local fisherman for nearly forty years. Llanelli-born Stewart Lloyd was in the Royal Navy as a radio operator, serving on *HMS Leopard* and the submarines *HMS Cachalot, HMS Finwhale,* and *HMS Opossum.* After ten years he joined the police force and was posted to Aberystwyth, where he met Christine, his wife-to-be, and they came to live in Borth. Dr Cynwy Davies, who served the local community for decades as a General Practitioner, was in the Royal Navy prior to commencing his medical studies.

This book covers only a small percentage of Borth's seafaring families and depends largely on material provided by their descendants. This leavens the work by making the stories, where possible, more human, compared to soulless statistics. It is tricky to disentangle links through marriage that connect many village families, making it impossible to isolate some family histories into neat chapters. An example is the Davies mariners of Maesteg House, who are entwined this way with the Lloyd, Enos, Williams, Herbert and Jones families. This collection of family and individual stories does not sit easily within chapters, so I have written them as a series of events, like a logbook recording a voyage through Borth's maritime history.

Seafaring was a hazardous occupation, exacerbated by conflicts. In World War One, 3,305 merchant ships were sunk with the loss of 17,000 lives. In World War Two, 4,780 merchant ships were sunk with the loss of 32,000 lives. Below is a list of Borth men who lost their lives during the two World Wars.

1914–1918
MERCHANT NAVY
Thomas Arter
Basil L. Davies
Thomas H. Dutton
William Hughes
Hugh James
Daniel Evan Jones
David Kenneth Jones
Hugh Jones
David Llewelyn Lewis
John Morgan Lloyd
Morgan Morgans
Thomas Richards
Llewelyn Roberts
Richard Rees
John Williams

ROYAL NAVAL RESERVES
Richard Davies

1939–1945
MERCHANT NAVY
John Hayden Ellis
Ieuan Griffiths
John Emlyn Herbert
Raymond Hughes
John Ivor Kinsey
Evan William Lewis
Thomas Lloyd
David Hughes Richards
Eric Robilliard
David John Thomas
William David Thomas
Peter Weldon
Evan James Williams
Howard Lloyd Williams

ROYAL NAVY
Fred Moore

There are two men missing from the 1914–18 Merchant Mariners List of lost Borth men. The first is William Jones (1847–1918), who was captain of the *Swan* in 1875 and later torpedoed on the *SS Dewa* in March 1918 whilst serving as first mate. Six months later, he lost his life when the *SS Rysdael* was torpedoed. The second, William Roberts, who had moved from Borth to Liverpool, was the nephew of Captain Hugh Jones, and with others from Borth, lost his life when the *SS Heathpark* was torpedoed in the last months of 1918.

Henry Levi Williams and Captain John Edwards lost their lives during the Spanish Civil War.

I would be pleased to receive any correspondence to do with Borth maritime history. Family histories and memorabilia would be acknowledged and added to an existing archive. Any photographs of ships and seamen would be of interest, and any paintings of sailing ships or steamers with Borth connections, which I could record photographically, would be greatly appreciated. All material would be treated with confidentiality. The author can be contacted by e.mail on mandersshaw@yahoo.co.uk, or by post at Brynowen Cottage, Clarach Road, Borth, Ceredigion, Wales, SY24 5LN.

The Daniel Family

The Daniel family first appears in the late 1700s, with sloop owner David Daniel the elder (1766–1850). In 1792 he married Catherine Lloyd, daughter of Jane Lloyd, a widow who lived at Penygraig farm. When Jane Lloyd died, she left the tenancy of the farm to Daniel and Catherine. However, Catherine died soon after her mother; David then married Elizabeth Davies in 1801, a widow from Nancwmlle. David and his two wives produced six boys and five girls. His children with Catherine were: David the younger (1793–1844), master mariner; Daniel (b. 1794, died as a child); Jane (b. 1796), and Evan (b. 1798), who became a surgeon. David's children with Elizabeth were Thomas (b. 1802), master mariner; Catherine (b. 1803), Mary (b. 1807), Alban (b. 1809), master mariner; Elizabeth (b. 1811), Anne (b. 1816) and David (b. 1818), who was first mate on Daniel-owned vessels.

David and Elizabeth's eldest son Thomas married Anne James of Brynllys in 1828 and their children were Thomas (b. 1829), master mariner; David (b. 1830), master mariner; James Watkin (b. 1833), master mariner, and Rosina (b. 1835). Thomas and Anne's son David married Jane Edwards, and their children were Anne (b. 1852), Jane (b. 1854), David Edward (b. 1858), master mariner, Thomas (b. 1860), Margaretta (b. 1863), Rosina (b. 1866), Richard Lewis (b. 1868) master mariner, James (b. 1870), ship's engineer, and Zezinia (b. 1873). Thomas ended up in New Zealand, where his granddaughter Betty Vodanovich still lives.

David Daniel the elder was owner and master of the *Amity* and the *Mary & Ann*. In 1838 he also bought the sloop *Linnet*, built at Aberdyfi in 1826, from Mary Jones, daughter of Anne and Morgan James, master mariner of Borth. Six years later it was sold to Richard Hughes of Gwastad, Borth. The registration was cancelled two years later with the vessel being broken up. These sloops carried limestone and culm to the Borth foreshore, where there were several limekilns. In the guidelines to parish boundaries two kilns are mentioned that stood near today's lifeboat station.

The Daniels were involved for a time with farming at Penygraig, which in the eighteenth and nineteenth century was part of the sizeable estate of Pengoitan Farm. The rent for Penygraig Farm in 1800 was £50 a year. It is likely that there was a limekiln on Penygraig farmland, down at Aberwennol beach. The Pengoitan estate ceased to exist as a land-owning identity by the beginning of the twentieth century, and is now a private house.

The seafaring family members eventually left Penygraig to live in Morfa Borth around 1840. However, Mary Daniel, daughter of David the elder and Elizabeth, married a farmer, Richard Jones, and stayed at Penygraig for another ten years, before moving to live at Tynshimne Farm. Her half-sister Jane, the third child of David the elder and Catherine, married William Jones, a farmer of Rhiwlas. They had five children, and the eldest Mary married Thomas Pryse of Bryn Bwl Farm in 1845. Their eldest son Thomas (b. 1846) became a master mariner in 1881, served on the *Lockton*, and lived with his wife Gwen at Glanwern.

The schooner *Francis*, built at Aberystwyth in 1816, was bought in 1824 by Thomas Daniel (1802–1836), the first Borth-owned schooner. The shareholders included Thomas' father, David Daniels the elder of Pengraig (38 shares), Enoch James (2 shares), David Morgan (2 shares), John Hughes (2 shares) and William Thomas the elder (2 shares); all mariners of Borth. Other shareholders included farmers John Rice of Tynllechwedd, John Jones of Tirhelyg and Evan Lloyd of Tydu Farm, who was a relative of Jane and Catherine Lloyd of Pengraig. Three years later, Thomas Daniel the skipper purchased all the shares from the other Borth shareholders. For a time after his death in 1836 his widow Anne, now a major shareholder, was signing documents relevant to the vessel's voyages. Captain Hugh Davies of Borth ran this schooner from 1838 to 1840; later her master was David Morgan of Gwastad, Borth. By 1855, Ann Morgan of Borth had acquired all 64 shares of the *Francis*, which, after trading for nearly fifty years, was lost with all hands on 3 December 1863.

The schooner *Aquila*, built in Penybont parish, Machynlleth, in 1833, was the Daniel family's next acquisition. Alban Daniel (1809–1840), fourth son of David Daniel the elder, commanded this vessel, and had 12 shares in her. His father owned 16 shares; Morgan Lloyd of Tydu Farm had 4 shares, David Hughes (4 shares), Thomas Daniel (4 shares), Richard Davies (4 shares), Evan Daniel (4 shares), John Parry Talybont (4 shares) and Rowland Evans Aberdyfi (4 shares), amongst others. Alban's half-brother Evan, although having gone to London to practise as a surgeon, still maintained a financial interest in the family's shipping concerns at Borth.

David Daniel the younger commanded the *Neptune, Hope, Linnet* and, briefly, the *Aquila*. His half brother David (b. 1818) was first mate on the *Aquila* as well as other Daniel-owned vessels. The Aquila changed hands on 3 February 1856, and five years later ended up wrecked on Aberystwyth beach. A succession of Borth master mariners commanded her at various times: David Hughes (1842), Thomas Richards (1844), William Jones (1845), William Williams (1850), William James, Tŷ Canol (1851), John Hughes (1852) and Enoch James the younger (1853). Captain John Hughes married David Daniel the younger's widow in 1846.

On the *Aquila's* final voyage from Saundersfoot to Aberdyfi, with a cargo of culm, she encountered a severe storm and had lost many of her sails by the time she rounded St David's Head. She ran with the southwesterly gale with just fore and aft sails all through the night and into the next day. Captain Enoch James (b. 1821) and his hard-pressed crew kept the crippled schooner afloat until they were driven ashore on Aberystwyth beach, where she was pounded in the surf. The crew were saved by eight local men who rowed out to assist, and by crew-members of the gunboat *Violet*, who waded into the surf with lifebelts and lines. This naval vessel was stationed at Aberystwyth, recruiting men for the RNVR. Everyone got ashore safely, and this particular incident bought about the establishment of a lifeboat at Aberystwyth. Captain James went on to own and command the schooner *Beatrice*.

A schooner built in Porthmadog in 1850 was purchased by the Daniel family, with James Watkin Daniel, master mariner, and his extended family running it. She was re-named *Rosina* after his sister. Another sibling, Thomas Daniel (1829–53), who previously captained the *Caernarvon*, commanded the *Rosina* briefly before dying of tuberculosis at twenty-four years old. The shareholders were Ann Daniel (8 shares), Abraham James Dolybont (8 shares), and Enoch Watkin James (8 shares).

Rosina Daniels, fourth child of Thomas and Anne, nee James, married two master mariners: the first, Captain Evan Evans of Borth, was drowned when the barque *South Walian* was lost with all hands near Venice in 1861. She later married Captain Thomas Watkin Humphreys in 1865. Captain Humphries lived in Aberystwyth in a cottage called Fairlina and was lost in 1875 on the schooner he owned, named – like his home – *Fairlina*. The *Rosina* was eventually wrecked at Holyhead in 1893. Rosina Daniels died in 1920 at eighty-five years old. Family descendants suggest that the name Rosina was of Spanish origin, as a member of the Daniel family had married into the Aberystwyth family of Delahoyde who originated from the Iberian peninsula. A Captain Delahoyde is buried at Llandre churchyard: his home is named as Borth. In the family history of the James' of Brynllys, there is a record of James, son of Morgan, of Llety Evan Hen, marrying a Rosina in 1729, the daughter of John De La Hoyde of Glandyfi.

David Daniel (b. 1830) of Osborne House, Borth, bought the barque *Bertie* in 1879. This vessel was built at Whitehaven in 1863 and was 140 feet long and 27 feet broad, with a male figurehead. The *Bertie* proved to be unlucky for the Daniels family. First of all, in 1883 David Edward Daniel (b. 1858), son of the owner, died whilst in command of her at the age of twenty-five, apparently drowned at sea in Latitude 8, Longitude 2. This vessel voyaged frequently to the coasts of West Africa and South America seeking cargoes of coffee beans. It was on a voyage to Brazil in 1891 that another tragedy struck when the whole crew and 61-year-old Captain David Daniel died of yellow fever. One Borth man, David Hughes (b. 1848) of White Lion Place, escaped this fate after serving on her as first mate for several years: he had left the vessel in 1888.

In the Aberystwyth registers it states that the *Bertie* was sold to Wilson & Sons Co. Ltd, who converted her into a hulk in the same year at Santos. This whole episode had a poignant sequel when later, Captain Richard Lewis Daniel (1868–1963), the sixth child of David and Jane, was invited ashore by some of the passengers of a Royal Mail Line vessel he was commanding. As they were finishing their pre-dinner drinks a bell sounded summoning the diners to the restaurant. The Captain instinctively recognised the particular sound, and as he passed, he looked at the bell: on it was the name *Bertie*. It was from his family's vessel, on which his brother and father had died, and had been salvaged when they converted the *Bertie* to a hulk.

Richard Lewis Daniel had an outstanding maritime career. There were mariners amongst his mother's family, with John Edwards (b. 1796) and John Edwards (b. 1819) both master mariners. By the age of twenty-three Richard had attained his master's certificate; his skills were so advanced that he passed a higher navigation examination and was soon on the Lloyds Captains' Register. In 1898 he was captain of the *Atrato*, and in 1900,

Captain Richard Lewis Daniel (1868–1963)

the *Tagus* and the *Arno*. He also commanded the *Carmarthenshire, Secura, Magdalena, Ekaterinoslau, Deseado, Oratavia, Agadir* and the *Caron*; troop and supply ships during the Boer War, for which he received a medal, and Red Cross ships sailing from France to the UK during the First World War. Whilst in the Royal Naval Reserve he carried the rank of commander and was involved in action at Scapa Flow. On retirement, if you could call it that, he was the chief marine superintendent of the whole of the Royal Mail Line, and was buried with this company's flag draped on his coffin at West Worthy, Sussex. He had mingled with royalty and 'captains of industry', as the many fine photographs in the collection of his granddaughter, Anne Jones of Aberangell, attest. Richard Lewis Daniel's career was the apogee of the talented Daniel maritime family of Borth. Fate, however, struck him a terrible blow as his only son, Richard Daniel, died a relatively young man. The only memento left is a photograph of him in his Naval Officer Cadet's uniform. Another of the captain's brothers, the seventh child of David and Jane, was James Daniel (b. 1870), who became a ship's engineer and lived in Liverpool.

This enterprising family had major shareholdings in several vessels, some of which they owned outright. The menfolk commanded at least a dozen local sailing ships: the *Amity, Hope, Dove, Linnet, Mary & Ann, Neptune, Active, Aid, Reform, Francis, Aquila, Rosina* and the *Bertie*. Captain R. L. Daniel, whose career was mainly involved with steamships, commanded over a score of vessels in an illustrious career up until the 1920s. The Daniels produced nine master mariners. The Daniel girls married into many other prominent maritime families in the area, such as the James, Edwards, Jones, Davies and Evans families of Borth, and the Humphreys and Delahoyde families of Aberystwyth. It is to be noted that it was David Daniel the elder and his second wife Elizabeth who produced generations of mariners.

Betty Vodanovich of New Zealand, a descendant of the Daniels, who provided much of this information, discovered during her researches that there was another maritime Daniel family in Borth, seemingly unconnected: David Daniel (b. 1805) captained the *Dove* in 1862 and the *Maria Anna* in 1865, a John Daniel (1823-58) was a first mate on local sloops, and another David Daniel (b. 1839) was the captain of the *Mary Jane*. In the 1871 census, this David Daniel was at Borth with his wife Mary and daughters Catherine, Emma and Margretta. The names of some of the children of the 'other' Daniels that appear on the census lists are sufficiently similar, such as Margretta, to raise the possibility that these two families are somehow related. Did David Daniel the elder have a brother from whom these other Daniels are descended?

The Jones Family
(Ffos y Gravel and Everton House)

At the beginning of the nineteenth century William Jones, master mariner, lived in Aberystwyth with his wife Jane, whom he had married in 1816. They had five children, and then moved to Newport, Monmouthshire, presumably seeking seagoing employment there. One of their sons, William Jones, born at Aberystwyth in 1829, married Mary Jones of Borth at Newport in 1854. Perhaps the Jones family of Aberystwyth had some relatives in Borth, as eventually son William and daughter-in-law Mary moved back there to Everton House. They had six children, three of whom were born in Borth. William Jones served as mate on the schooner *Picton* and sailed to Mediterranean and Spanish ports. He later captained the *Picton*. On his marriage certificate, it stated that he was a master mariner. He features in a group photograph of Borth master mariners, circa 1890.

William's wife Mary Jones was one of five children of John Jones, master mariner, of Ffosygravel Farm, Borth, who commanded several vessels including the sloop *Neptune*. Mary's brother Thomas Jones (b. 1823) was also a master mariner, who at one time had been in the Royal Navy, serving from 1850 to 1856 on *HMS. Albion*, *Louisa* and *Waterloo*. He received a Crimea war medal that was once proudly displayed at Pilgrim House, Borth. After his war service he passed his master's certificate in Dublin in 1860, and from 1866 to 1875 he owned and captained the *Pilgrim*. The captain's residence in Borth was named after this ship, but when his two spinster daughters, Elizabeth and Mary, retired there, where they gave piano lessons, they apparently got so fed up with being teased by being called 'The Pilgrims' that they changed the house's name to The Glyn. The *Pilgrim* and the *Picton* were, at one time, very much Jones vessels, the latter lending its name to Picton Terrace, and later Picton House.

One of William and Mary's daughters, Mary Jane Jones (b.

1856), married master mariner Evan Hughes (1849–1882). Unfortunately he died of liver disease whilst at sea shortly after they were married, and there were no children from this union. He became captain in 1874, and commanded the sailing vessels *Hannah* (1874-77), *Hugh Ewing* (1877-79) and *Spirit of the South* (1879-82). Mary Jane later married another Borth master mariner, David Williams (1849–1910), and had two children, of whom only the daughter Elsie survived; the son Edgar died in infancy. Another daughter of William and Mary, Annie (1862–1928) married master mariner Evan Jenkins (1859–1900), whose brother David was also a master mariner.

Evan Jenkins (b. 1859) gained his master's certificate in 1888 at Liverpool. He commanded the barques *Rose Hill* (1889-92), *Holt Hill* (1892-96) and *Bidston Hill* (1890–1900). His brother David Jenkins (b. 1848) became a captain in 1877, but unfortunately died in an accident on board the *Nant Francon* in January 1882 at Mostyn, north Wales, the ship having just arrived with a cargo of iron ore from Bilbao. The inquest reported that David had become entangled in the machinery of a steam winch and suffered fatal head injuries. Their sister, Annie Jenkins, married John Arter (b. 1854), another master mariner, who commanded the *SS Carron Park* in 1888.

Mary Jane and Annie had two brothers, William John (b. 1857) and Thomas (b. 1859), both of whom became master mariners and for two decades were associated with the Hill Line Co., Liverpool. This company, owned by Thomas Pryce of Workington, ran a fleet of some of the largest sailing ships in Britain. On his first voyage William John Jones went with his uncle, Captain Thomas Jones, Ffosygravel, on the brig *Pilgrim* to Taragona. Later he became second mate on the barque *Glendovey*, captained by John Williams of Borth, on a voyage from London to Rangoon, then passed as master at Liverpool. William John went to sea at the tender age of twelve, and had nineteen voyages prior to becoming second mate on the brigs *Pilgrim*, *Glendovey* and *Ocean Belle*, and the schooner *Picton*, which were all Borth vessels. He was later master of the sailing vessels *Ellen Greaves, Spirit of the South, Ethel Anne, Douglas Castle, May Hulse*, and then the *Bidston Hill* (1891–1898) and the *Holt Hill* (1898–1901). The *Ellen Greaves* was a Caernarfon-registered 254-ton brig, with an all-Borth crew in 1881. Captain Jones circumnavigated the world many times.

On one voyage, in the summer of 1894, the *Bidston Hill* carried a dangerous cargo consisting of 20,000 cases of petroleum. This substance had already accounted for many ship losses, as its lethal explosive potential was not yet fully realized. Captain W. J. Jones had loaded the ship at New York, which was then bound for China. To make the voyage even trickier, the large barque ran aground near the entrance of the Yangtze River. After carefully transferring the 20,000 cases into lighters, the three tugs successfully towed the vessel free. It was on this vessel that John Davies Maesteg gained his second mate's certificate in 1893 under the guidance of Captain W. J. Jones. There is a fine photographic montage of the *Bidston Hill* and its crew, featuring the previously-mentioned John Davies and also another John Davies of Glen Rosa; both went on to become captains. In 1906 the *Bidston Hill* sank with all hands off Cape Horn.

The owners of the Hill Line, the Pryces, had kept faith with Borth captains, who proved more than capable of handling their large sailing vessels, as none were lost with these men in charge. Consequently, some of the Pryce family visited Llwyn Glas Farm whilst on holiday at Borth in the 1920s, out of respect for Captain Jones and his family.

Captain W. J. Jones married Mary Owen (1835–1905); she looked after her two brothers John and David at their home at Cerrig Y Carrannau Isaf. The captain lived there for a time when he was home from sea, and after his wife Mary's death moved to Everton, Borth, to live with his widowed sister. His son and wife once joined him in America, and returned to Britain via Hamburg on the *Bidston Hill*. The captain eventually went to live in Tal-y-bont just prior to his death in 1929. His brother Thomas Jones, named after his Ffosygravel uncle, became mate in 1880 and passed as master in 1883 at Liverpool. He was soon to command the *Rose Hill* (1885–1888) and the *Mow Hill* (1889), and was lost at sea on 24 January, 1890, at latitude 19 longitude 27 west.

Another descendant was Captain Emrys Jenkins (1894–1975). He was born at Gordon Villa, and educated at Borth County School, and later at Machynlleth County School. Despite having the ability to pursue a scholastic career, he chose instead to go to sea at the age of fifteen, on a three-masted barque captained by his uncle, John

Arter, who according to family lore, refused to mollycoddle him. By 1920 he had gained his master's certificate and thereafter captained steamships. From 1929 to 1944 he was master of the *Thala, Batna, Brika, Marsa, Kerma, Hamla, Modavia, Fort Crevier* and *Fort Spokane*.

Newly-weds Captain and Mrs Emrys Jenkins

He was involved in both world wars and lost the *Fort Crevier* in Bombay on her maiden voyage from New York when a nearby American munitions vessel exploded, causing extensive damage and killing over 500 people. He also lost £100-worth of presents he had bought for his wife in New York just before sailing – a large amount of money at the time. He hardly ever spoke about his maritime activities, other than to say that his experience of the Second World War, despite the previously mentioned explosion, was a picnic compared to that of the First World War. Emrys continually told his wife that he always sailed in convoy with an escort of Royal Naval warships. This was true, but what she did not know was that 20 miles out they went off on other duties. Towards the end of the Second World War a torpedo explosion damaged his hearing to such an extent that he retired to become a farmer at Commondale in Yorkshire. His daughter was apparently named after a ship he once commanded, the *SS Sheila*.

These six Borth families, namely the two Jones', Jenkins', Arters, Williams' and Hughes', were interconnected, and as a glance at their family tree shows, there are a score of seafarers; mostly master mariners. It seems that mariners from these intermingled families voyaged predominantly on large sailing ships from deepwater ports. Indeed Emrys Jones, the provider of this large and at times complicated history, mentioned that his grandfather, Captain W. J. Jones, loathed steamers, and considered their captains and crews to be second-class seamen.

A tragic story concerns another of Emrys Jones' family, his cousin David Nathan Bunce Morgan (1916-40), the son of James and Gwen Morgan of Llandre. Like his father he was a gifted medical practitioner and became a Surgeon Lieutenant in the RNVR during World War Two, serving on the *HMS Gurkha*. He was involved in the Norwegian Campaign. Apparently the captain of the ship pre-empted orders, resulting in the vessel being attacked by the Germans. The crew was kept on the ship from 9 am until 6.30 pm, before taking to the boats. For many of them, including David, it was too late. He is buried at Trondheim Cemetry, Norway. His father was understandably furious as well as upset, and believed that they should have abandoned ship sooner.

The Jenkins Family
(Alma Place and Rock House)

There were other maritime Jenkins families in Borth, one of whom is mentioned in the preface in connection with Sophia Jenkins (1872–1959). Master mariner David Jenkins, (1788–1874), was born at Gwastad, had a long career about which little is known. However, we do know he had two master mariner sons, David (1814–1905) and John (1820–1878). David who lived at 1 Alma Place, commanded the *Hope* (1856-8), *Osprey* (1859-66), *Sarah Davies* (1867–68) and for the last two years prior to his retirement, he was mate on the Nerissa. He was pensioned off in 1880. His brother John commanded the schooners *Hope* (1860–63), *Lady of the Forest* (1870–76), and *Glad Tidings* (1876–78). He died at fifty-eight years old, leaving a widow, Anne, who lived at 2 Alma Place and drew a pension until her death in 1891. He is buried at Garn Cemetery.

In 1861 the sloop *Osprey* had an all-Jenkins crew, with David (b. 1814) as master, his sons David (b. 1840) as mate and John (b. 1843) as deck-hand. David (b. 1840) became captain in 1868 and commanded the *Glencaple* (1871–76), by which time he was living at 28 Portland Street, Aberystwyth. He was captain of the *Nerissa* for the ten years until 1889, and his next command was the schooner *Hope*. In 1892 he drowned when this small local vessel was caught in a hurricane off the coast of Canada.

His brother John (b. 1843) also became a master mariner and lived with his wife Phoebe at Rock House. They were to have several children, one of whom, David Jenkins (b. 1870), became a ship's engineer and was one of the survivors of the sinking of the *SS Cadeby* in 1915. David's three brothers all joined the church: Llewelyn became a Canon and Thomas and John William were vicars. The latter was named after his cousin John William, Sophia's brother, who died at eighteen months of age in February 1874. Thomas had the privilege of playing association football for Wales on two occasions. He was picked for the national team a third time, but the Bishop of St. Asaph would not allow him time off, and he was not asked to play for Wales again. Another Borth man, William Morris of Brynrodyn Farm, played rugby union twice for Wales in the 1960s.

There were two cousins at sea around 1870: one was Thomas Jenkins of Rock House, on the *Lady of the Forest*, and Richard Jenkins, the son of Thomas and Rebecca Jenkins, who was lost at sea in 1874. Another relative, John Jenkins (b. 1840), was captain of the sailing vessel *Fairy* in the 1870s, with fellow villager Thomas Williams (1844-73) as first mate.

Captain John Jenkins (1820–1905) had a master mariner son named David (1846–1883). He had married Jane, the daughter of William James. David died relatively young at thirty-seven years old in 1883. The couple lived at Windsor House, which belonged to the retired William James. They had only two children: a son, John William died in infancy, thus ending this branch of the family's maritime involvement. Only the daughter Sophia survived.

Captain David Jenkins (b. 1846) was master of the brigantine *Agenoria* and the schooner *Sophia & Emily*. He was part-owner of the

Captain David Jenkins (1846–1883), captain and ship-owner

latter, as well as having shares in several other vessels. The *Sophia & Emily*, built by Messrs. Jones & Williams of Aberystwyth, was launched in 1873 by Miss Emily Lloyd at a grand ceremony. This vessel had a figurehead of twin sisters. Unfortunately only two years later the vessel had to be abandoned at sea. Quirkily, Captain Jenkins' final voyage was back on board the *Agenoria*, which was under the command of Captain Hugh Hughes (b. 1827). Although Captain Jenkins died of tuberculosis at Jarrow, Newcastle upon

Tyne, he is buried in the family grave at Garn Cemetery, Llandre. Two years after he died, the by-then-ageing *Agenoria* was condemned and sold by order of the Court of Admiralty in 1885.

Captain Lewis Jenkins owned and commanded the barque *Dorothy*. On his death in 1871 his widow Ann became sole owner and employed her nephew Captain John Jones to run the vessel. Captain Jenkins' fourteen-year-old son Lewis Jenkins (1857–1909) was the ship's boy on the *Lady of the Forest* in 1871. He went on to become a master mariner. In 1889, he married Sarah Anne Roberts, daughter of William Roberts, Cambrian Terrace. He served on many vessels including the *Hero*, and died of acute dysentery in 1909 whilst captain of the *Byron*.

The Arter Family

The Arters were another family with a long maritime history. Captain William Arter (1818–1854) commanded the schooner *Aberystwyth* and drowned in October 1854. John Arter (b. 1839) was mate on the schooners *Mary & Ellen* and *Sarah & Mary*. Later, another William Arter (b. 1843) sailed as ship's boy on the schooner *Eliza Francis* before becoming captain in 1871, and for a time master of the schooner *Cambrian*. He had served as mate on the *Margaret Lewis* and the *SS Mountpark* and later as second mate on the *Sir Galahad*. His brother David (b. 1846) was a ship's boy on the schooner *Reform*, with Borth's John Williams (b. 1823) as captain. David went on to gain his captaincy in 1875 and commanded the Mountpark with his previously-mentioned brother William as first mate, and another brother Enoch (b. 1849) as bosun. William David Arter was recorded as being a fifteen-year-old cook on the schooner *John Pierce*, captained by John Hughes of Borth.

There were also brothers William John Arter (b. 1873), first mate, and William Llewellyn Arter (b. 1874), chief engineer. William Llewellyn spent most of his career working for Manchester Liners Ltd and served on the *Manchester Brigade*, *Manchester Hero*, *Manchester Division*, *War Pundit*, *Manchester Citizen* and *Manchester Progress*. He was at sea for over fifty years throughout both World Wars. A cousin, Thomas Arter (b. 1880), another ship's engineer, died in World War One on the *SS Harbury* when she was sunk by the German submarine U70 in June 1917 whilst on a passage from Buenos Aires to Brest with a cargo of grain. Thomas' brother David (b. 1883), who rose to the rank of second mate, died at the age of thirty-six as a result of an accident on board the *SS Charios*. The vessel was docked at Port Talbot: a heavy block fell on David's head, killing him instantly. These two brothers lived at Bay View. This family had moved to Manchester by 1900.

The Lewis Family

Families bearing the surname Lewis produced over two dozen mariners during the nineteenth century. There were a clutch of mates, beginning with Lewis Lewis (1810–67), on the schooner *Elizabeth Ann*; William Lewis (b. 1827) on the *Eleanor Francis*; David Lewis (b. 1829) on the schooners *Estella* and *Lizzie*; Abraham Lewis (1844–71) on the *Amy Serena*, the vessel on which he died at Bahia Brazil; Humphrey Lewis (1862–1913) who died whilst serving on the steamship *Don Cesar* and David Lewis (1870–99) who died whilst serving on the *South Cambrian*.

The captains begin with Rees Lewis, who commanded the sloop *Sincerity* in 1803. John Lewis (1822–87) commanded the schooners *Jane & Sophia*, *Ceres*, *Cecil Brindley*, *Alcazar* and the *Electra*. Thomas Lewis (1832–64) passed as captain at thirty years old and commanded the schooner *Jane Owens*. Evan Lewis (1833–88) captained the *Rachel Lewis* and then served as mate on the *Lady Jozyn* and the *Artizan*. He died on the latter vessel and is buried in Buenos Aires. John Lewis (b. 1836) commanded the sailing vessels *Margaret Lewis* and *Snowdon*; and later the steam sail vessel *Nant Gwynant*. John Lewis (1845–81) became captain in 1872 but served as mate on the *Zulette* where he was dismissed for the harsh treatment of a crew member. He eventually captained the schooner *Volunteer* for three years until his death at Queenstown in Ireland.

Thomas Lewis (b. 1845) commanded the sailing vessels *Cambrian*, *Seiriol Wyn* and the *Snowdon*. Richard Lewis (b. 1848) captained the *Bootle*. Enoch Lewis (b. 1852) passed as master when he was only twenty-one years old. He was the son of the previously mentioned Captain John Lewis (b. 1822), and went to live at Aberdyfi two years after gaining his captaincy. Another Captain John Lewis (b. 1857) commanded the *Archimies*. Thomas Lewis (b. 1860) was master of the *Nesta*. William David Lewis (b. 1867) was mate on the barque *Snowdon* prior to gaining his captaincy. He went on to command the steamers *Boltonhall, Grantleyhall, Hendonhall, Derwenthall, Lindenhall, Siltonhall* and the *Stanwell* over a period of thirty years from 1900. Evan Morgan Lewis (b. 1869) became captain in 1896 and commanded steamers throughout the First World War, including the *Annie Hough* and the *British Coast*. The Lewises also produced two ship's engineers, John Lewis (b. 1865) who served on the *Seroun Prince*, and John Benjamin Lewis (b. 1876).

The Edwards Family

The Edwards clan produced half a dozen master mariners, primarily in the nineteenth century. Edward Edwards (1822-86), who became captain in 1865, took over command of the barque *Walton* on which he had previously served as mate. From 1874 to 1882 he was in command of the barque *Eurydice*, then captain of another barque, the *Robert Kerr*, on which he died after serving two years. Thomas Edwards (1846-99) passed as captain in 1880 after serving as mate on the *Fairy Queen*. There is no record to date of vessels that he may have commanded, but he served as first mate on the *Mirella* in 1887, and later the *Celtic Chief*, the vessel on which he died. Richard Edwards of Glanwern (1851–1910) gained his captaincy at the tender age of twenty-one, and commanded the sailing vessels *Convoy, Florence* and the large barque *Holt Hill.* John Edwards (b. 1875) became a captain in 1904. In a forty-year career at sea he commanded the *Graffoe, Carronpark, Hazelpark, Wellpark* and *Beechpark.*

Another John Edwards (b. 1887) also had a long seafaring career working his way up the ranks. By 1912 he was second mate, then first mate in 1916, and a year later master. He was known locally as Captain Edwards Penybont. He was master of the *SS Stanwell* for two years until she had to be abandoned in a sinking condition with no casualties in 1934. This small 425-ton vessel ran into a fierce gale whilst carrying a cargo of coal from Barry Dock to Figuiera Da Foy in Portugal. The chief officer at the time was 58-year-old Borth man John Taylor. Unfortunately John Edwards lost the *Plas Dinam* in the same year off the coast of Newfoundland, with another Borth man Rowland Ellis amongst the crew. Captain Edwards was in command of the steamer *Nicolaos Baekas* in the 1930s, but did not survive the decade as he was killed during his involvement in the Spanish Civil War. John Ivor Edwards (b. 1903) became master in 1930 at twenty-seven years old. He had some narrow escapes during the Second World War; one ship, the *Mountpark* was sunk by enemy gunfire in

1940. He commanded the *Grangepark*; his next vessel, *Ocean Freedom*, was bombed in port. He was highly commended for war services, and continued at sea after hostilities, commanding the *Hollypark*, which was in collision with another ship in dense fog near the South Goodwin Lightship in 1947.

The Hughes and Jones Families

Captain Hugh Hughes (b. 1827) commanded the sloop *Dart* (1857–1860), the sloop *Bee* (1870–1872), the schooners *Martha James* (1872–1874), *Lady Zetland* (1875–1877), *Agenoria* (1881–1883) and the *Clara Felicia* (1884–1886). He amassed quite a property portfolio, owning and at one time living in Gwendon, and later resided for a time at Tynparc in Llandre. He owned three cottages built around 1700 (to the south of the Railway Inn at Borth), which he left to his daughters. The centre one, Hendre, was where one of his last descendants, a granddaughter, lived. His older brother, Captain John Hughes, was born in 1823, lived at Llandre, and captained the schooners *Capricorn* and the *Jane*. The Hughes clans produced fifty or so seafarers, with over twenty master mariners, and were primarily active in the nineteenth century.

David Hughes (b. 1825), was master of the 99-ton brigantine *Malvina*. Another David Hughes (b. 1841) became a captain in 1865, and commanded the local sailing vessels *Mary Anne, Ivanhoe* and, for a decade, the 663-ton barque *Caroline Spooner*. Evan Hughes (b. 1849) was captain of the barques *Hannah, Hugh Ewing* and the *Spirit of the South*. He died on the latter vessel leaving a widow, Mary Jane Hughes, who lived at Everton House.

There were four John Hughes': one, born in 1808, was captain of the *Aberystwyth*, another, born in 1823, captained the

Ship's captain and property-owner Captain Hugh Hughes (b. 1827)

schooner *Jane* of Aberystwyth. A third, born in 1834, drowned at sea while captain of the *Jane Maria* on a voyage from Vera Cruz to London, and a fourth John, born in 1836, owned and commanded the local schooner *Lorne* for over twenty-five years. Disentangling the relationships of the Hughes families of Borth is almost impossible. They and the James' crop up everywhere, marrying into other seafaring families such as the Daniels, Ellis', Williams' and Jones'.

Members of the James family of mariners feature throughout this book. They not only commanded ships, but owned many, still remembered in the Borth house names Gleanor, Beatrice, Resolute and Dovey Belle. Enoch James (b. 1787) became a master mariner. John James (b. 1813) was master of the *Resolute* and the *Dovey Belle;* Richard James (1815-93) commanded the *Aberystwyth*. William James (b. 1820) commanded the sailing vessels *Aberystwyth, Island Maid, Ocean Belle* and the *Dorothy*, and eventually went to live in Aberdyfi to be near his shipping interests. He owned the barque *Glendovey*, which was ably commanded by his nephew John Williams. Another John James (b. 1845) was master of the *Dovey Belle* in 1881. John Hughes James (b. 1855) served on the *Miniera* and in 1904 was a sub lieutenant in the RNR He went on to be the master of Park vessels such as the *Wellpark* and *Mountpark,* and lived at Richmond House. Captain John James (1875–1932) served on the *Western Coast* and the *Dolphin:* he died on board the *Dolphin* at Falmouth on 29 August 1932.

The Davies Family (Maesteg House)

Captain John Davies (1872–1947), of Maesteg House, Borth, was one of the most loved characters of the village: kind, considerate and a supreme optimist who worked all over the world in far-flung places. For five years he was trading from the ports of Shanghai and Hong Kong, and later worked on the Eastern seaboard of Canada and America, as well as plying the Great Lakes. He was a classic example of a seafarer who took the transition from sail to steam in his stride. He was a great entrepreneur who owned sail and steam vessels for nearly forty years.

His grandfather, John Davies, born in Tresaith, married a Borth girl and settled down in the village. They had five children, one girl and four boys, John, William, Enoch and Thomas, who all went to sea by the time they were nine years old, on coastal sloops. Unfortunately John Davies and three other Borth men were caught in a sudden storm whilst herring fishing in the bay, and they all lost their lives. The three eldest boys died before their thirtieth birthday, leaving Thomas to support his mother and sister. Thomas went to sea with Captain Richard Jenkins from the port of Aberdyfi. Later he obtained his master mariner's certificate at Dublin when he was twenty-two years old.

Thomas, now firmly established, married Margaret Williams, who came from Ysbyty Ystwyth. They had five children, Margarita, William Thomas, John, Enoch and Evan. The boys were named in remembrance of Thomas' brothers who were lost at sea. Evan was the only son who did not go to sea, and became vicar of Llandrillo, Merionethshire.

William Thomas Davies (1869–1934) went to sea at thirteen years old on the barque *Dora Ann* of Aberystwyth. On this first voyage, he went to the west coast of South America under the command of his uncle Captain John Lloyd. Afterwards he sailed in schooners and steamers, both in the home and foreign trade. He obtained his second mate's certificate in 1890 and his master's three years later. He was on the *SS Glanystwyth* as Second Mate, then first mate on the *SS Glanhavren*, remaining on her until he gained his master's certificate. At twenty-five years old he was captain of the *Glanystwyth* and the *Glenveck*, which were owned by Mathius Co. of Aberystwyth. He stayed with this company until they sold all their ships in 1922. He managed to sail throughout the Great War without mishap, despite some very narrow escapes.

William Thomas supplied provisions for the Dardanelles Campaign, and was at other times under charter to the Cunard Company, and also the French Transatlantic Line. He captained the *Cheltonian, Etonian, Carthusian, Rugbeian, Cliftonian, Clan Keith, Northern* and the *Plas Dinam*, on which his first officer was Ieuan Griffiths of Minfor House, who later tragically died in World War Two on the *SS Hamla* of London. The captain's only son, Gwilym Idwal Parry Davies, after completing his engineer's apprenticeship at Vickers of Barrow, served as an engineer officer with the Blue Funnel Line, where he obtained his first engineer's certificate. Later he took up a shore appointment with Texaco Oil Company in Liverpool; as soon as World War Two broke out he joined the army and became a major in the Royal Tank Corps.

Enoch Davies (1876–1923), who lived at Grosvenor Villa, became a blacksmith at the Eagle Foundry, Aberystwyth, and after receiving his indentures, joined the *SS Glanhavren* as third engineer. Promotion followed, and he joined the *SS Feliciana* as second engineer. In 1900, he gained his first engineer's certificate whilst he was back on the *Glanhavren*. During one of the voyages on this vessel a propeller was badly damaged some distance from Bermuda. Calling on his experience as a blacksmith, he welded pieces of metal to form a clamp around the shaft. After waiting for the seas to calm, and flooding the forward tanks to raise the stern, he went over the side with a spare nut and got the propeller back into position, and secured the whole system. This time-consuming operation unfortunately took its toll on him and he was left in a very weak condition, affecting his health thereafter.

During the Great War, Enoch was torpedoed twice, the second when he sailed with Captain J. O. Enos on the *SS Cheltonian*. After the war, his brother John persuaded Enoch to go halves in the *SS*

Cornubia, which traded with John in command, and brother Enoch as chief engineer. This vessel ended her days wrecked on the Irish coast on a voyage from Galway to Ayr in Scotland. A terrific gale sprang up and as she was in ballast she could make no progress against the heavy seas. Consequently the vessel drifted beyond control onto the Mantle Rocks, 15 miles off Galway. The crew of ten landed near the village of Inveran. A large number of the locals boarded the ship and looted all that they could lay their hands upon. Sadly, and rather ironically, Enoch drowned in Gloucester Canal on 27 March 1923.

Captain John Davies (1872–1947) went to sea at the age of thirteen on the schooner *Jane Owen*, owned and commanded by

Captain John Davies, Maesteg (1872–1947), known as 'John China' because he had captained ships in the Orient

Captain Richard Jenkins, who was at this time well into his seventies. This was remarkable as both John and his father before him went on their maiden voyages with the same skipper. John sailed in many vessels of different types, and obtained his second mate's certificate in 1893 on the barque *Bidston Hill*, with Captain William John Jones of Borth in command. Finding the next berth was very difficult as there was a slump in shipping trade at the time.

Eventually he joined the *SS Alma* and went on to serve as second mate on the *SS Earl of Dumphries* and *SS Glantivy*. He then moved back to sail on the large barque *Lord Shaftesbury*, and became first mate on this ship serving in that capacity from 1897 to 1899. He later joined the

China Navigational Company Coastal Service to Shanghai, and remained with the company until 1910, before returning home, gaining his master's certificate in 1902.

John Davies married Margaret Catherine Ellis, daughter of gamekeeper Hugh Ellis from near Dolgellau. Their daughter Meiriona Ellis Davies later married Captain Lewis James Herbert. Mother and daughter joined the newly-appointed captain in Shanghai, and lived for three years in Havelock Street. Granddaughter Jean Caswell relates that on many an occasion they had to admonish their Chinese nanny who kept binding infant Meiriona's feet in the time-honoured tradition, and simply could not understand why they kept undoing her well-intended bindings. Apparently Meiriona's feet were troublesome for most of her life.

It was from his sojourn in the Orient that John Davies got his nickname John 'China', as he had captained the *Klukiang* and the *Foochow*. Whilst at Shanghai he met other Borth captains who were employed there for a time, Thomas H. Dutton (1865–1915) and Captain David Thomas of London Cottage. After John Davies' return, he was appointed captain of the *Margam Abbey*, which was owned by Williams and Morley of Cardiff, a company that he remained with until the end of 1916, when this ship was torpedoed in the Bay of Biscay. He and the crew, which included Borth men, Rowland Ellis and John Davies of Trigfan House, were landed safely at Barry by the Italian steamer *Antonia Silesia*. By 1918, he was engaged in what was euphemistically termed 'work of national importance'.

Captain John Davies was continually involved in ship ownership – sail and steam. In fact, as late as 1920 he was buying schooners. One, the *Brandon*, was sunk by enemy fire in 1918; another, the *Industry*, was wrecked on the Irish coast in 1921. After that he concentrated on steamers, and as is mentioned in Captain L. J. Herbert's memoirs, his father-in-law, Captain Davies, took his own vessel, the *Myrtis*, to work on the east coast of Canada and the Great Lakes, where in winter they often had to dynamite their way through the ice. When dense fog enveloped the St Lawrence Seaway the fog horn was sounded; its echo was timed to gauge if they were still in the middle of the seaway.

According to Captain Herbert, who was then first mate on the

Myrtis, part of the cargo taken from Canada to the United States was alcohol – this was during the time of the American prohibition. Captain Herbert later made his own son-in-law, Ken Caswell, swear not to relate the nature of that particular cargo to Mrs. Herbert (the daughter of Captain Davies), as she would be mortified: the family was strictly teetotal. Apparently, to the initial mystification of First Mate Herbert, they docked at 3 am at an unscheduled berth. Suddenly warehouse doors opened: out stepped men wielding firearms. In the dim light provided, the cargo, cases of alcohol, were quickly unloaded. Doors were closed and the armed men melted away. The ship then moved to arrive at their designated berth to unload a legitimate cargo. Captain Davies had obviously cast a convenient blind eye over that particular cargo as the proceeds went towards a successful business sojourn in Canada that ended up with him purchasing land in Newfoundland. Captain Herbert's daughter Jean relates that some of this land was sold to the Canadian Government to facilitate road-building, but there is still some left which the family would like to sell off.

Captain Davies was founder member of the Borth Sea Scouts and taught the youngsters navigation. Borth carnival benefited from his enthusiastic support and organisational skills. He was a fine vocalist; at the reunion of the Master Mariners of the counties of Cardigan and Pembroke in June 1937, he is listed on the programme as singing eight solos, mostly were shanties. At this same gathering Borth's Captain Richard Jones also sang a shanty.

The Thomas Family

For three centuries there have been Thomas mariners at Borth. John Thomas was commanding the sloop *Bee* in 1783; Thomas Thomas ran the sloops *Cambria, Wonder* and *Success* in the 1820s. Evan Thomas, who ran the sloop *Active* in the same period. Another Evan Thomas (1805-77) became a captain in 1851 and commanded the schooner *Lydia*. He married Anne James in Llanbadarn and they had ten children, one of whom, John (b. 1848), was mate on the *Wellington* and the *Rheidol Queen*, before becoming a master mariner. He captained the local schooner *Volunteer* throughout the 1860s. When John was on the *Wellington* she won a race against another local vessel, the *Hope*, from Darien to Aberystwyth with a cargo of pitch pine. One of John's sisters married into the notable Clayton maritime family of Aberystwyth.

Master mariner William Thomas (1770–1841) married Mary Jones (1772–1852). Their son David (b. 1817) became a mariner; he married Anna Maria Roberts (1816-46), a farmer's daughter. Tragically Anna died twelve days after giving birth to a son, William Thomas (1846–1908), who served as mate on the sailing vessels *Nellie, Cassia, Janet & Mary, Eleanor, Charlotte, Helena, Messenger, Jane Herbert* and the *Cantheus*, gaining his master's certificate in September 1868. Forty years later he drowned in the North Sea whilst serving as second mate on the steamer *Kirkwall*. He had married Jane Jones in 1873, daughter of Captain John Jones and his wife Margaret. One of their four children, John David Thomas (1875–1900), was lost at sea when the *Ocean Belle* sank with all hands off the coast of Denmark.

Other seafaring Thomas' were Edward (b. 1830), who was mate on the brigantine *Helen* of Newport in 1861, and Thomas Thomas, who was master of the 134-ton schooner *Naiad* of Llanelli. Another descendant, Captain David Thomas (b. 1870) of London Cottage, was for a time in the Orient where he often met up with Captain John Davies of Maesteg House. Captain Thomas was employed by a company in Australia when World War One broke out. He took command of the *SS Kinross,* bound for the UK. As he approached British waters in May of 1917, a German submarine ordered them to the boats and sank their vessel. He and his crew landed safely at St Ives, Cornwall. Captain Thomas went on to command the *SS Seistan* (1921–24); in the 1930s he was master of the *SS New Mathilde.*

The Rees and Davies Families
(Arequipa, Angorfa, Trigfan)

The Rees clan provided seamen for over 200 years. They appear in historical records beginning with Captain John Rees (b. 1752), who commanded the sloop *Providence* in 1774. His son Thomas (b. 1790) commanded the same vessel in the 1820s, then his father took over running her in the 1830s. The *Providence*, built at Garreg in the Dyfi estuary, was owned by this family for over fifty years. John Rees had also captained the sloop *Liverpool Trader* in the 1830s. His grandson, another John Rees (b. 1820) captained another family-owned sloop, the *Mary Rees* in 1842, and then went on to command the schooners *Falcon* (1857), *Miss Evans* (1863) and *Acorn* (1864). Enoch James, who commissioned the schooner *Beatrice* in 1862, sold it to Thomas Rees, master mariner, in 1884. Unfortunately two years later she was lost off the Irish coast. Twelve years later, as a result of this loss, Captain Rees was declared bankrupt, demonstrating the perilous nature of ship ownership.

The Rees girls of Angorfa Cottage married into other

Richard Davies, known as 'Dic Trigfan' after his home in Borth

seafaring families. One married Captain Thomas Davies of Mariner's Cottage, later Morwylfa. Their son Abraham Davies had two girls and three boys. Of the daughters, Ginny became a nurse and went to live in London, and Maud became a primary school teacher. All three of the Davies boys became mariners. Richard, known locally as 'Dic Trigfan', had served as a young soldier in World War One but was invalided out in 1918 suffering from typhoid. From 1919 to 1929 he was at sea serving on the *Southern, Mecklinberg, Ciscar, Beechpark, Manhattan, Hazelpark, Tabora, Clytha* and the *Dalblair*. He then became a civil servant, working in the Ministry of Agriculture and Fisheries.

John Davies was at sea most of his life. He was torpedoed three times in the Second World War. The last time saw him severely injured and he spent over two years convalescing in a Montreal hospital. He never really recovered and became rather withdrawn, and spent the rest of his life working as groundsman at Borth Golf Club.

Tommy Davies was a ship's cook and lived at Pantgwyn. I remember him performing in one of A. E. Richards' nautical plays at the Borth Public Hall. He had served on the South Wales Borderers in World War One, and on demobilisation he worked at Borth Bakery. After a time the flour affected his lungs and he had to seek other employment. Tommy, like his brothers, turned to the sea and became a ship's cook. His son Jeffrey, who provided this information, was the only Borth man who served in the Korean War, and afterwards embarked on a lifelong career in the police force.

Jeffrey mentioned there were letters kept by his parents which were written by three Rees mariner brothers whilst away at sea: this correspondence was about planning the building of three cottages taking advantage of the *tŷ unnos* system. These were today's Angorfa, Morfan and Sabrina. Unfortunately these priceless documents were deposited with a solicitor on the death of Jeffrey's parents, and were lost.

Shan Dudleston, 'Dic Trigfan's' daughter, remembers her father telling her that his cousin Ivor used to be sewn into his underclothes when winter arrived and was only freed in spring. Sadly Ivor was a casualty of the First World War, and one of the few remaining photographs of him was taken with his grandparents outside the

Rees family home, Angorfa. The Rees mariners had a long association with the *SS Dingwall*.

Another of the Rees clan, Captain David Rees who lived at Gloucester House, now Caer Gwyddno, owned and commanded the barque *Drusus* for a two-year period before his untimely death in 1881. His wife Elizabeth became the owner; she mortgaged the vessel for £280. Her joint mortgagees were Margaret Thomas, Tan yr Allt Farm, and Ann Davies of Tal-y-bont. The vessel was sold two years later at Rosario on 8 November 1883.

Captain David Rees (b. 1828) gained his master's certificate at twenty-six years old. He captained the sailing vessels *Eleanor Francis* in 1860, *Sarah* in 1862, *Helena* in 1864, *Rebecca* in 1866, *Edith* in 1875 and the *Sabrina* in 1885. In 1891 he was master of the 73-ton schooner *Kate* of Chester, a vessel with only three crew: the sixty-four year old captain, fifty-year-old mate Thomas Hughes, and a twenty-year old able seaman, William De Lydes of Plymouth. David Rees often took his young son Thomas (1845–1915) with him on these vessels. David Rees named his cottage Sabrina after the schooner, and later, on adjacent land, his son Thomas built a large house that he named Arequipa.

After becoming a master mariner in 1879, Thomas Rees was involved in importing timber from North

Captain Thomas Rees (1845–1915), who built the large house named Arequipa in Borth

America to build this new home for himself and his wife Elizabeth Jane. He went to sea at fourteen years old and for thirty-three years was master of ships belonging to the Hough and Coast Lines, such as the *SS La Tamice* and the *Edith Hough*. He never had a mishap, and in the time-honoured tradition, the directors of the company gave him a sumptuous farewell dinner. Captain Thomas Rees applied to be nautical assessor in 1907, two years after tragedy had struck when his only son, Glyn Owen, died of tuberculosis in 1905 whilst attending Shrewsbury School. At Captain Thomas Rees' funeral in 1915, his pallbearers were those who had sailed with him or were connected to the Hough Lines, including my great-grandfather, David Davies of Balmoral House. Only a daughter, Dilys, remained, who did not marry and lived on in the family home. It was the end of a long maritime succession.

The only photographs of this family are courtesy of Hazel Jenkins. Hazel looked after Miss Dilys Rees prior to her death and was given, and rescued, a few mementos from the many that were destroyed during house clearing. Nancy Birch, and others who visited Miss Rees, remembers there being a large collection of ship's photographs on the walls of Arequipa. Some belonged to the shipping company associated with Nancy's forebears.

Other Borth captains at one time or another worked for Coast Lines, amongst whom were Captain Thomas Williams, Francon House; Captain Thomas Davies, Gloucester House; Captain Herbert, Ger y Don House; Captain E M Lewis, Glan y Don House, and Captain John James, Dovey Belle House, the latter as marine superintendent.

Another Rees mariner, David Hugh (1892–1962) was a ship's engineer who married Annie Bertha James, the daughter of Captain Hugh James. He served on the *Thistlemore*, *Ardgroom* and the *Invertay*. They lived at Grassmere, but strangely on his headstone he is memorialised as a 'Captain', although I cannot find any record of him being anything other than a ship's engineer.

The Richards Family (Maelgwyn)

Captain William Richards (1845–1912) gained his master's certificate in 1872 and commanded the sailing vessels *Cecil Brindley* (1873), *Martha* (1874–1879) and the steamers *Glenalvon* (1879–1882), *Eira* (1882–1883) and the *Lady Mostyn* 1883–1888). He began his career as ship's boy at twelve years old; at sixteen, he was a seaman on the sixty-ton *Aberystwyth*, registered schooner *Maid of Merion*. He then went on to serve on the *Forest Princess, Punch, Forest Queen, Annie Brocklebank* and the *Mary Elizabeth*; all sailing vessels. He was one of eight children. His brothers David (b. 1841), John (b. 1848), Thomas (b. 1852) and Evan (b. 1855), all became mariners. Of the three sisters, Megan (b. 1853), Jane (b. 1850) and Ann (b. 1858), only Jane married a mariner. The captain's father John (b. 1819) was a mariner, but on some documents he was noted as a farm labourer.

Captain Richards was from a large clan of Borth mariners that had produced, amongst others, a Hugh Richards (1733–1807), noted on his gravestone as a mariner. Captain Thomas Richards (b. 1822), who passed as captain in 1850 and commanded the schooner *Tirsah* (1859–1873), and later the steamer *Lady Mostyn* before his retirement in 1880. There was also Captain David Richards (1835–1873) who was captain in 1865 and commanded the *Edward John* from 1865 to 1867. Captain David Hughes Richards (b. 1879) of London House had a narrow escape in 1901 when he was second mate on the SS *Herschel*, when she was run down by the SS *Ardeola* in thick fog. David gained his captaincy in 1905 and commanded the *Wellpark, Mountpark, Dawnpark, Holmpark* and *Rowanpark* throughout World War One. He was on the *Grainton* as first mate in the Second World War, well in to his sixties. Other relatives, John and Elizabeth Richards of Tanygoitan Cottage, lost their twenty-year-old son Edward John when he drowned after the sloop *Conductor* was wrecked on the Kish Bank. It was John and Elizabeth who helped persuade Captain William Richards to buy a parcel of land on the cliff pastures of Pengoitan Farm to build two houses, namely Maelgwyns 1 and 2, in 1903. There were also distant relatives at Aberdyfi, one of whom, Captain David Richards, commanded the schooner *Maglona* which was lost with all hands on her maiden voyage off Cape Race, Newfoundland, in the 1870s.

Captain William Richards had four children. His elder son, John Thomas, became a ship's engineer, but unfortunately drowned when the boat on which he was returning to his ship was driven hard against the vessel's side, throwing him overboard. After this tragedy the other son, David, was forbidden to go to sea and became a carpenter. Several letters found recently in Maelgwyn Pengarn's attic, by the current owner Richard Gethin, are from *Eira* crew-members William Hunt and John Graham. They indicate that the captain's two daughters, Peggy and Mary Elizabeth, and their mother, had gone with their father on the maiden voyage of the *SS Eira*. According to his descendants, Captain Richards did not entirely trust this vessel in bad weather, and indeed his fears were borne out when she later vanished on a voyage between Whitehaven and Kronstadt in 1898.

Also among these letters are some from Richard Williams, a schoolteacher from Borth, who at one time courted Mary Elizabeth. In them he complains that despite blowing a whistle at intervals to signal that he was near her home at Pengarn, she did not come to meet him. This romance did not progress, as she later married a Davies from nearby Aberceiro. Mary Elizabeth and her husband moved to London where she became the first female sanitary inspector in Britain. She was also an active suffragette and closely associated with Emmeline Pankhurst's inner circle.

The captain's son David, who had been forbidden to go to sea, had two sons, the eldest of whom did go to sea. Edward 'Ted' Albert Richards (1904–1981) was in the RNVR during World War Two. He attended Towyn Grammar School where he excelled academically. Despite this he was not happy there, and walking out onto Towyn beach to look south to Borth, often ending up crying. Ted went on to take a degree in chemistry at the UCW Aberystwyth, but decided that he would prefer to be in the arts than the sciences. By 1928, he was in London in a book-retailing partnership. Times were quite lean in the 1930s, and he took on bit-part acting jobs and began writing plays. Many of these were abstractions of Borth's historical associations with the sea, such as *Master Mariner, Who'll Buy My Fresh Herrings* and *Herring Harvest.* Overall, he wrote twenty-four plays and a few short stories, some of which were later re-drafted and presented on radio.

At the end of 1941, with the war reaching a crucial state, Ted decided to do his bit and joined up. It was natural that he would join the navy, but his age dictated that it would be in the RNVR. He was soon promoted and found himself involved with training exercises on minesweepers. Ted often remarked about the comical mix of the crew on these vessels. Most of the skippers were trawlermen in peacetime, who knew the coastal waters in and around the English Channel like the back of their hand. These rough-and-ready men, now uncomfortably uniformed, were trying to organize hapless officer recruits from public schools and the professions, who had no sea-going experience. Other than his sea-going duties, Ted, because of his background, was given liaison duties, looking after the welfare

A. E. 'Ted' Richards (1904–1980), playwright and sailor

of new recruits and organizing sporting events and theatrical entertainments.

Ted often recalled that on one busy recruiting day when he hardly glanced at the procession of new faces, as he called out 'name and address etc' a small voice replied *'Ted bach, fi sydd yma; rhwyn perthin i ti'* ('Dear Ted, it's me here, I am related to you'). It was ship's cook Llew Jenkins from Borth, who had found out where Ted was stationed, and had come to invite him to share some food he had smuggled ashore. Trite a story it may seem, but Ted often recalled it wistfully. Llew took him to his rented room high in the attic of a London house, and on a little gas ring cooked a sumptuous feast of bacon and eggs. This was something very rare at the height of rationing; as Ted stated, 'Thank God the skylight was opened so the aroma would not attract attention'.

Some descendants of this branch of the family had only tenuous links with the sea. Ted's son Paul (b. 1944) ran inter-island vessels as part of his brief when District Officer in the Solomon Islands in 1970. He then returned to Britain and taught at HMS Arethusa for a time. After emigrating to Australia in 1976 he pursued a teaching career, and is currently, in his retirement, a member of the Australian Volunteer Coast Guard. Ted's brother John Thomas, 'Jac', named after his long-lost ship's engineer uncle, has a son John (b. 1946) who served for thirty-five years in the RAF; a daughter Ann (1942–1995) was married to David Morgan who went to HMS Conway and was for a time an officer in the Merchant Navy.

Captain William Richards' great-grandson Thomas Davies (b. 1937), descended from William's suffragette daughter Mary Elizabeth Davies, decided to go to sea when he was about five years old. He got up in the attic at Maelwgyn Pengarn for the first time alone and found, rolled up in a basket, a watercolour of the *Lady Mostyn*, his great-grandfather's last command. From that moment on, he decided he was going to be a seafarer. After matriculating at fifteen years old, Tom set about going to sea and signed up with the shipping federation who vetted prospective apprentices. He went to King Edward VII College in Whitechapel for three months of pre-sea training. From there, he was expected to find his own shipping company. Just after the war, with shipping decimated, tanker companies such as BP as British Tankers, and Shell, were recruiting apprentices. Their ploy was that as tankers were at sea for longer periods than dry-cargo ships, one's apprenticeship would be over quicker, therefore becoming an officer much sooner. Tom agreed to join BTC (British Tanker Company).

Capt. A. J. R. Williams of Cardigan was the only Welsh skipper Thomas Davies ever served with. As Tom says, 'A man completely without fear and a great skipper, he always had me at the wheel as soon as we picked up the pilot, somewhat to the chagrin of some ABs. I believe I was a good helmsman and never let him down.' Tom joined his first ship, the *British Diligence*, in Swansea, BTC's homeport. Even though tankers went to most parts of the world, the crews saw very little of it: a full shipment of oil could be discharged in a couple of days and loaded at some terminals in 24 hours.

On Tom's last trip on a tanker, he spent a fair amount of time on the bridge. Tankers were dry, no liquor, so shore trips meant that crews drank copious amounts quickly and got very drunk. Tom, a non-drinker, remembers leaving port a few times with only the apprentices, the 'sparks' and the cook fit to 'let-go'. Tom served on a dozen ships and travelled, as he says, 'most of the seas, some benign, some ferocious'. Laden tankers were the least affected by bad weather, but in ballast were much higher out of the water, making it difficult. On one trip to Australia, fully loaded, Tom's ship was caught in a typhoon. He remembers being excited, but quite a few on board donned lifejackets. Tom served on six tankers: *British Diligence, British Councillor, British Diplomat, British Ranger, British Harmony* and *British Skill*. During his apprentice days, when he had time off, he would be at Borth, staying with relatives Jac and Maisie Richards, and working at the Welsh Kitchen Restaurant.

After getting his ticket, Tom joined the Royal Mail Line, as he was attracted to the idea of voyaging to South America. At this point his father presented him with his grandfather's sextant – it was an old Vernier type and very different from the new ones. Tom took it with him and used it – despite the funny looks the first time he took a noon sight, it was just as accurate as anyone else's. Tom's first ship with Royal Mail was the *Highland Monarch*, a cargo passenger ship on the Brazil River Plate run carrying outward passengers in three classes. It had the mail contract for the South America run and delivered and collected mail from all the ports it stopped at: La Coruña, Vigo, Lisbon, Las Palmas (Canaries), Recife, Bahia, Rio de Janeiro, Santos, Montevideo and Buenos Aires. Tom was mail officer and hardly got ashore, as the ship would arrive early in the morning and sail late in the afternoon. The main cargo was chilled beef, freshly killed sides, hung in timber lined, cork-insulated holds, high enough to allow the sides of beef to clear the decks. They were packed just tight enough to not allow them to swing about in bad weather yet not packed so that they ground together and damaged the meat. The temperature had to be maintained at between 33 and 34 degrees Fahrenheit. There were engineers aboard whose sole job was to ensure that the temperature never varied so the meat stayed at the 'as-killed' state for the thirty days it took to reach London.

Tom made four trips on the *Highland Monarch*, then joined the *Parima*, a cargo ship, also refrigerated, for one trip. He then joined the *Alcantara*, the second-largest of the Royal Mail fleet, the *Andes* being the flagship. The *Alcantara* carried about two thousand passengers in the three classes. Tom was very pleased to find a gymnasium on board; although mainly for passengers, he was allowed to use it. He was a member of the Earlsfield Boxing Club, at that time one of the most successful in the country, and keen to make the top grade. He had promised his trainers that he would work very hard while at sea. Approaching Brazil, Tom started to feel ill with flu-like symptoms. This continued for a couple of days, which ended in him having to report repeatedly to the doctor. Finally he was told the shattering news that he had polio. It was his worst nightmare. He ended up in the ship's hospital; upon arrival at Rio he was transferred ashore. There was quite a panic, as an officer had died on board with polio some time before. After a few months Tom was declared fit enough to be flown back to the UK. He was lucky to be alive, but the polio caused the loss of most of the muscles of one leg,.

Tom had to convalesce at the Dreadnought Seamen's Hospital in Greenwich, and for a time, post-hospitalisation, became a ship-keeper. When a ship arrived home and the officers were due leave, ship-keepers would 'keep ship'; keeping the log, overseeing cargo and so forth. Tom soon declared himself fit and went back to sea, first on the *Albany*, then the *Durango*, part refrigerated and part dry cargo. This latter vessel was John Lloyd of Borth's old ship. Meat was still the main cargo, but occasionally they carried oranges and potatoes, and voyaged between Britain, South Africa and South America. Tom did five trips on the *Durango*, and on the last trip met his wife-to-be, Maruchy, who was amongst the passengers. After getting married, Tom resigned and went to work with the Lotus Car Company. Tom has done many things including sailing the Atlantic and serving on the *Winston Churchill* as a Watch Officer. He lived for over a decade at Ardwyn House.

The Jenkins Family
(Gordon Villa and The Elms)

Captain William Richards' sister Jane (b. 1850) married local mariner Evan Jenkins, and one of their sons, John Richard Jenkins, and his wife Elizabeth, produced two mariner sons, Thomas 'Tommy' Richard Jenkins and John Llewelyn 'Llew' Jenkins. Whilst Tommy was serving as Chief Steward on the *Lylepark* in the Indian Ocean during World War Two, the ship was torpedoed by a German submarine. The survivors, including Tommy, were handed over to the Japanese and spent the rest of the war in a prison camp. The authorities knew nothing of his fate. He was named a war casualty. His wife Edith received an official death notice from the king. A few years later, lo and behold, Tommy was pronounced alive and on his way home. Edith went to London to meet him, and he was also given a rapturous welcome by the villagers who went to meet him at Borth Station. Tommy became a postman until his retirement. Tommy's brother John Llewelyn, 'Llew', was at sea all his life as a cook, and served on the *Clunepark, Broompark, Empire Star, Empire Highway* and the *Mahia*. In 1946 the *Mahia* was in Australia for a time with a skeleton crew, but Llew decided to move ashore to St Kilda, Melbourne, and was posted as a deserter .

Ship's cook Llewelyn Jenkins

During the Second World War, Llew had a very narrow escape when he was on the Denholm Line cargo ship the *Clunepark*. This ship was part of a nineteen-vessel convoy that sailed from Freetown for Liverpool in January 1941. Twelve days later, 200 miles south-east of the Azores, an unidentified cruiser steamed into the centre of this convoy. Suddenly she identified herself as the German battle cruiser *Admiral Hipper*, rapidly sank six ships, and badly damaged three others, then slipped away. The *Clunepark* was only damaged, but in the confusion it was assumed that she would soon sink. It was then decided that some members of the crew should transfer to another cargo vessel, the *Blairathol*. Borth men John Thomas and his brother William were part of the evacuation, but Llew elected to stay on board the damaged vessel because he could not swim. Tragically, William Thomas died along with seven others in the confusion of the transference. Every time I saw Johnny Thomas, who was the local painter, I would immediately recall the story of how he could hear William desperately calling for his brother to save him in the dreadful oil fire that broke out immediately after the attack. It is ironic to think that if those eight men had stayed on the *Clunepark*, there would have been no fatalities. Llew and other crew-members managed to get the *Clunepark* safely to Madeira.

Llew had two sons: the elder, David, joined the army; Richard followed family tradition by joining the Royal Navy, serving for over a decade. He was on the *HMS Duncan* in 1962 in the North Atlantic. He was on *HMS Albion* (1964–1968) as part of the Far East fleet; he was in the home fleet (1970–1972) on *HMS Antrim*, touring the Mediterranean.

It was inevitable that ship's cook Llew Jenkins would bump into other Borth men. He once met up with steward Elvyn Williams of Hyfrydle, in a bar in Vladivostok of all places, and they drank and sang the night away. Elvyn and his brother Harry were at sea in the 1930s. They were the sons of the local chemist who took a series of remarkable photographs of old Borth captains around 1900. Elvyn was captured by the Italians and became a prisoner of war in Timbuktu, North Africa. After the Italian surrender, he was quickly repatriated due to ill health; after recovering he became a civil servant until his retirement.

The Jones Family
(St Clare and St Albans)

David Jones (1838–1932) was one of six children born in Borth to a Welsh-speaking family. His father, also David Jones, was a mariner, and his mother, Jane Rees, came from Wallog, daughter of a fisherman who lived in one of the two cottages which were later demolished to make way for today's Wallog House. Young David was much abused at school over his failure to speak English, and with great relief left at an early age.

His parents secured a job for him as a cabin boy on a ship voyaging out of Caernarfon. At the tender age of nine, David made the long walk from Borth to Caernarfon, involving two ferries across the Dyfi and the Mawddach, and an overnight stop in Porthmadog, all presumably arranged in advance: an overall journey of approximately 50-60 miles, depending on the route taken. He would have kept mainly to the coastline before walking over the hills from Porthmadog to Caernarfon on the second day, for which an early start was essential if he were to reach his destination by nightfall.

The ship he joined had a surly, miserable crew and barely edible food. He hated it so much that when the vessel returned to Caernarfon he hid until it set sail again rather than go back on it. The ship was subsequently sunk with all hands in a storm off Bardsey, but some months later the local newspaper reported that David Jones' trunk had been washed up on the beach; it was recognised by the inscription in the Welsh Bible discovered inside it.

By then David had found a much better ship, and his seafaring days began in earnest. In 1861 he was on the local schooner *Jane Owens* as an able seaman. He was certified mate in October 1865, and sailed in that capacity, on the brigantine *Xanthus*, to Spanish and Italian ports; this vessel was later lost on the Goodwin Sands. He became captain in 1868, and from then until 1870 commanded the *City of St. Asaph*, voyaging to Australia and South America. He captained the *Elizabeth* for a number of years: a Russian 'prize ship', brought back as booty from the Crimea. This ship was probably re-named after his elder sister, grandmother or mother-in-law, who all bore the name *Elizabeth*. This vessel was a regular on the lucrative run from Mostyn to Coruña with a cargo of slate, returning with iron ore. Some Welsh ships coming into port from a long voyage would have a ship's song, to be sung very loudly by the crew, so that those waiting to greet them would identify the vessel. The *Elizabeth's* was a popular tune they had picked up in Spain, known today as the hymn 'Madrid', or the 'Spanish Hymn'. In 1875 he was captain of the *Tamaulipas*, which was his last command prior to his long commitment to the steam yacht *Ceres*.

David Jones married a local girl, Margaret Williams, in 1863, when she was twenty-four. Her father was Captain William Williams (1811–57) who was a master mariner by 1851, and commanded the schooners *Jane & Mary* in 1855 and the *Hypsipyle* in 1857. The latter was lost at sea with all the crew in November 1857. Captain Williams' antecedents were all mariners. Margaret's mother was Elizabeth Simon, whose brother, Captain John Simon the elder (1807-81), owned and ran the sloop *Robust*, built at Aberarth in 1832, which was eventually lost in 1855. He had commanded the schooner *Adelaide* in 1861, and amongst the all-Borth crew was his son Simon as ordinary seaman. Later, he reverted to mate on the *Adelaide* at sixty-four years old, when it was under the command of John Hughes. Apparently, he had been deaf for the previous twenty or so years. His son, John Simon (1843–1917) became master mariner in 1870, and commanded the *Cuerero, Ellen Catherine, Sultannina* and the *Sulliana Reina*. His last command was the 79-ton Caernarfon-registered schooner *Ellen Roberts*. Interestingly, whilst he was captain of the *Sultannina*, the fifteen-year-old cook on board in 1880 was fellow villager Thomas Hughes Dutton, who went on to become a master mariner.

Margaret's four brothers John, Thomas, Henry and Richard were all mariners. John Williams (1841-79) captained the *Clara* and the *Agenoria*. They had lived in Aberystwyth, but after John's death she moved back to Borth, to Providence Villa. Margaret died a few years later. By 1891, their children were living either with David and Margaret Jones at St. Clare, or in the Friendship Inn: Margaret was the sister of David Hughes, the landlord, known locally as Dafydd y Friendship.

Thomas Williams (1844–73) was mate on the schooner *Fairy*. Henry Williams (b. 1846) began his career on the 67-ton Borth schooner *Resolute*, commanded by John James (b. 1819), and later became captain of the *Elizabeth*. Richard Williams (b. 1849) was mate on the same vessel, which was owned for a decade by their brother-in-law, Captain David Jones. Richard and Henry lived with their families in Mostyn, north Wales, where Richard built a house called Borth Villa. Another possible Williams descendant was second mate William John Williams (b. 1890), who served on the *War Isis, Siward, Denpark* and the *Norah Elsmie*.

In 1875, John Lancaster introduced Captain David Jones to the Duke of St Albans. From then until the Duke's death in 1898 Captain Jones commanded the 88-ton steam yacht *Ceres* on its numerous voyages, often to the Scottish Lochs, the Orkneys, Norway, the Holy Land and other parts of the Mediterranean. These voyages usually followed Cowes Week and lasted two months at a time.

Captain Jones had prior connections with Cowes, as for a short time he served as mate on the steam yacht *Rose*. A letter from him to his wife Margaret mentioning this fact was discovered recently in St Clare by Diana Logan. The *Ceres* was a regular fixture in Cowes Week, and became a focal point for visiting royalty. Famous royal names who went aboard at one time or another include Queen Victoria, the King and Duke of Montenegro, the Prince of Wales (later King Edward VII), Prince Leopold, the Duke of Orleans, the Kaiser, the Duke of Connaught, the Marquis of Shetlands, the Duke of Devonshire, Lord Lansdowne and many others. On the commoners' side, there were also Gladstone, Thomas Edison and Guglielmo Marconi. In 1881, Captain David Jones took his wife with him on a voyage to the Mediterranean.

Captain Jones used to make copious quantities of cold tea to drink in the hot Mediterranean climate. The Duke used to drink this as well, and both men were amused to find how much better they coped with the climate than those partaking of alcoholic beverages. There were gifts, too: a diamond tie-pin from Prince Leopold, a gold watch from the Duke of Orleans, a silver teapot inscribed 'To Captain D. Jones from Alfred Farquar', numerous gifts from the Prince of Wales and a watch from the Count de Morny. The Count was close to Napoleon III, who was himself an RYS member from 1858 to 1872.

Oddly, Captain Jones was never officially a contracted employee – he and the Duke shook hands and that was enough, ensuring he and his family were well provided for. In 1880, the captain's family lived at St Clare House, together with his older sister Elizabeth, who was a domestic servant, and her dressmaker daughter Jane. Captain David Jones then built three houses in his home village – appropriately 1, 2 and 3 St Albans – which stand today. David and Margaret Jones lived at No. 1, with daughter Moyra and sister Elizabeth. The captain's son Thomas, and his wife Amey lived at No. 2 with children David Elwyn, John Leslie and Amey Aerona. David's daughter Jane, and her husband Thomas Evan Williams, lived at No. 3, with son David Edwin. St Albans No 3 was passed on to their granddaughter Peggy. Peggy was married to Will Owen, for many years the stationmaster at Borth.

Captain Jones had the reputation of being firm, but fair, and was greatly respected by the crew. The original crew was from north Wales and Merseyside, but by the 1890s they nearly all came from the south coast of England. Captain Jones used to recall with affection a certain Billy Butt, who was first mate for a while. His sister was Clara Butt, the singer. The Butt family hailed from Southwick, near Brighton, Mr Butt senior was a sea captain himself.

After the Duke's death in 1898, Captain Jones was authorised to keep anything he wished from the *Ceres*, and the ship's contents were duly distributed among the members of his family. The forty-year-old vessel is believed to have been broken up shortly afterwards. It is unclear whether Captain Jones may have taken the opportunity to retire at sixty, or continued to worked on his own behalf for a while longer. His wife Margaret died in 1906, and in the 1920s he moved in with his youngest daughter, Moira, at Newtown, where she lived with her Methodist minister husband David Eglwys Jones and the first seven of their eventual eight children. By all accounts Captain Jones lived a happy life until he died in 1932 at the age of ninety-five. He made a famous journey from Newtown to Borth by bicycle when he was eighty-five. This is a journey of over 43 miles, which even today takes an hour and a quarter by car.

His eldest son, Captain William D. Jones (1865–1912), died at

sea and was buried in Malta. He was second mate in 1886, first mate
in 1887 and captain in 1890. He commanded the *Loango, Monrovia,
Ethiopian, Montpellier, Yola, Montfort, Mount Royal, Montreal, Lake
Simcoe, Montezuma, Lake Michigan, Radiance, Date Grove, Cassia,
Ainmere* and *Canadian Transport*. He lived at Montfort, named after
one of his ships. It was on this vessel that he took cargoes of
ammunition to South Africa at the beginning of the Boer War. For
his services Captain W. D. Jones received a cannon ornament made
from one of the first shells fired in the conflict. In a 22-year career he
safely captained sixteen ships. One wonders how many more he
would have sailed if he had not died at forty-seven years old. His wife
Elizabeth is buried at Pen-Y-Garn where there is also a memorial to
William.

Thomas Jones (1870–1957) was the second son of David and
Margaret Jones of St. Clare. Seafaring was in his blood, his father,
both grandfathers and several uncles all being mariners. At the age of
fifteen, he went to sea on a sailing ship, the *Ocean Belle*, at a wage of
fifteen shillings a week. By this time he had met his future wife,
Amey-Jane Lewis. Amey's grandparents, Hugh Jones (1805–43) and
Jane Thomas (1810–49), were born in Borth and lived at Tre'r-ddôl.
Hugh captained the sloops *Sincerity* in 1826 and the *Victory* in 1829.
His brother Richard (b. 1791) captained the smack *Picton*, the sloops
Brittania and *Mary Ann* and in 1840, the schooner *Brittania*.

One of Hugh and Jane's daughters Elizabeth (b. 1842) had
married a John Lewis and emigrated to America in 1874, when
Amey, their daughter, was two years old. However, Amey was sent
back back to Borth to attend school by 1882, after her mother's
death and her father's remarriage. Amey was bought up by her
mother's sister Susannah (1839–1916), who was married to John
Williams (b. 1838). They lived at Epworth House. John was mate on
the *Ocean Belle, Ceres* and *Bernina*.

Amey was two years younger than Thomas, and was a friend of
his younger sister Jane. After their first meeting, they began a lifelong
romance, which initially was kept hidden from friends and family. In
January 1887, Thomas set off on a long voyage on the barque
Snowdon to Australia, and Amey started to write a 'secret diary' to
record all her thoughts and feelings whilst he was away. Every day he
was away was marked off on a tally sheet she had prepared. Amey

Captain Thomas and Amey Jones

*Entry in Amey Jones' autograph book
from early in 1887*

wrote how she checked the *Gazette* for his sailing times from Liverpool, which was Saturday 15 January. She was constantly worried about whether he would start to smoke and drink, or worse still, meet someone else. None of these happened. Amey described how lonely she was without him and how frustrating it was to be unable to tell anyone. Amey left gaps in the diaries, in case they – and her passion – were discovered. The diary petered out in February 1887, probably due to the pressure of exams coming up, which she eventually passed to became a music teacher.

Amey's uncle and aunt had moved to Barry in Glamorgan, and so it was there that she and Thomas married two days before Christmas in 1896. Although Thomas and Amey's first children were born near Liverpool, the family moved back to Borth in 1901 to St Alban's Villas, built by Thomas' father. As previously stated, different members of the Jones families lived in the three houses. Thomas and Amey moved many times during his maritime career, living in Wales and the border counties, but after retirement, he moved to Rhyl, and when Amey died in 1943, he moved to live with his son at Connah's Quay, where he died in 1957.

Thomas had a long and varied career, starting in sailing ships and then gravitating to luxury passenger liners. He ran away to sea on the Borth-owned *Ocean Belle*, and then joined the *Snowdon*, another sailing vessel associated with the village, and voyaged to Australia and round Cape Horn to Valparaiso. He then joined the barque *British Army*, which fought its way for three weeks round Cape Horn and then took a hundred days to arrive at Portland, Oregon.

He was on the barquentine *Bootle*, carrying copper from Africa to Swansea, then on the *SS Alexander Elder*, voyaging to Baltimore, America. He gained his second mate's certificate from Liverpool in 1890, and voyaged to the Persian Gulf in that capacity in 1891 on the *SS Glantivy*. This vessel bought back a cargo of 5,000 tons of dates. He was first mate by 1892 and gained his master's certificate in 1894 at twenty-four years old. He then waited for five months to get a good post.

In 1895, he joined the Dominion Line and was an officer on the *SS Labrador*, and then on the *SS Canada* on her maiden voyage across the Atlantic to Montreal. Little did he know that he would later command her. He was First Officer on the *SS Dominion* and by 1900 he was captain of *SS Roman*, a cattle and freight steamer. He was one of the youngest captains crossing the North Atlantic at this time. After commanding the *SS Cambroman* and *SS Englishman*, he then became captain of the *SS Turcoman*, for fifteen years from 1903 to 1918. From that time, he became captain of the *SS Haverford*, a White Star Line ship. He was now in the luxury liner business, transporting people rather than freight. He later commanded the *SS Pittsburgh, SS Canada, SS Megantic, SS Cambroman, SS Doric* and *SS Regina*. When the *Pittsburgh* crossed the Atlantic on her maiden voyage in 1922 she was the first liner to be fitted throughout with electricity.

During the First World War the *Turcoman* was refitted and used to transport troops and horses as well as supplies. Captain Thomas worked out that in the two years 1915–1917 he had travelled 112,323 miles, and transported 6,694 horses and 2,866 mules. He remarked that the mules were much better sailors than horses. With

Captain Thomas Jones on the Turcoman, which he captained between 1903 and 1918

the *Turcoman*, he trans-ported some of the 7th Division to Zeebruge in 1914, when the siege of Antwerp took place. He crossed the Atlantic many times during the conflict and in 1918 was quoted in the American newspaper, *The Philadelphian*, 'I have been dodging subs since 1914 and I mean to keep on dodging them until the Kaiser gets tired and quits'. He had several encounters with German submarines, and possibly sank one by ramming it.

Captain Thomas Jones took part in three rescues for which he received honours. In 1908, as captain of the *Turcoman*, he rescued thirty-five French fishermen from the *Bearn et Bretagne*, which had lost its masts: for this he received a pair of fine binoculars from the French government and the Liverpool Humane Society's Silver Medal. Then as captain of the *Haverford* in 1918 he picked up the emaciated crew of the Norwegian ship *Augvald*, who had been adrift for eleven days in an open boat after a submarine attack, with no food and little water. For this he was rewarded with a silver trophy from the Norwegian Government.

Thomas' third rescue was in 1922 as captain of the *Pittsburg*, when he saved forty-five crew-members of the Italian ship *Monte Grappa*, whose cargo had shifted dangerously during a violent storm. For this the Italian government wanted to award him the Order of the Knight Grand Cross of the Italian Crown. However, the British Foreign Office would not allow it as it had a rule against foreign decorations being bestowed on British subjects. He did however receive a silver medal from the Liverpool Humane Society, the Life

Saving Benevolent Association of New York's Gold Medal, and a Diploma from the Italian Crown.

The rescue of the crew of the *Monte Grappa* was testament to his exceptional navigational expertise and seamanship. Thomas had to steam 260 miles on a course that he estimated would intercept the Italian ship at a point roughly 100 miles from where she had sent out the SOS. The *Monte Grappa* was being pushed by a severe storm at the rate of 8 knots, but as she travelled and wallowed deeper in the seas, she was reduced to a speed of 3 knots. All this Captain Jones had taken into account; as well as the time that the two ships would meet. They sighted each other within the hour predicted, and the *Monte Grappa*'s rockets were sighted off the starboard bow, as expected.

The Italian vessel, with Captain Bartoli in command, had been bound from Montreal to Venice, with a cargo of grain. The ship was caught in a huge southerly gale, and was fighting enormous cross-seas when the 9,000 tons of grain moved dramatically as the shifting boards gave way. There was a huge list to port, which gradually became worse, despite flooding the starboard ballast tanks in an attempt to even her up. The port lifeboats were washed away and the starboard ones could not be launched as they now hung over the decks. When the ship rolled in the heavy seas, her port light disappeared.

Two boats were launched from the *Pittsburg* into rough seas on a dark night. The passengers viewing the drama expected the *Monte Grappa* to roll over at any minute. The boats returned with forty-two of the crew, and one returned again for the captain, mate and chief engineer, who had tried desperately to save their ship. The only difficulty encountered in this incredible rescue was getting a 360-pound Italian man onto the *Pittsburg*.

A description of Captain Thomas Jones is provided by an American newspaper: 'The captain is becoming so well known to Philadelphia, that we begin to claim him as our own ... passengers which are carried by him claim that he is one of the most efficient and trustworthy men who have guided them across the blue seas'. The captain retired from the sea in 1927, but at the age of 82, was cruising on the Cheshire Canals with his grandson in his cabin cruiser Amey, named after his beloved wife. He died in 1957 and is buried at Keswick, alongside Amey, who had died in 1943.

The Williams Family
(Auckland House and Picton)

A miner, Lewis Williams (1815–91) and his wife Anne (1816–95), of Borth, had seven sons, one of whom a Thomas (b. 1842) died in infancy. Four of their six surviving children became master mariners. The first son, Captain William Williams (1839–1922), was associated with schooners *Picton*, *Mary Davies*, *Martha Lloyd* and the barques *Aberystwyth Castle* and the *Caradog*. In the 1881 census Captain Williams was master of the *Mary Davies*, berthed at Milford Haven, and under his watchful eye were his sons, John as first mate at seventeen years old, and Lewis, a cabin boy of thirteen. These two also served with their uncles on sailing vessels, providing them with the seagoing skills that eventually resulted in both becoming master mariners.

Lewis and Anne's second son, John Williams (1841–92), gained his master's certificate in 1870. By 1871 he was captain of the brig *Naomi*, which voyaged to the Mediterranean and South America. In the 1871 census, John Williams was master of the *Naomi* at thirty years old, and on board was his twenty-three year old brother Thomas Williams (b. 1848) as bosun.

After four years on this vessel, John Williams spent the next seven years in command of the barque *Granville*. He named his daughter Anne Granville after this ship. (I remember her as an old lady living in Auckland House.) Captain John Williams then commanded the barque *General Picton* until 1890. This vessel was lost in mid Pacific –not in a storm, but because the cargo of coal had self-ignited, and she burnt and sank. Luckily, the crew was rescued.

None of the captain's sons went to sea, but the eldest, John Llewelyn, who left Britain to take up a banking position in America during World War One, was for a time presumed lost on the liner *Appam*. For a time this vessel was posted missing, as one of her wrecked lifeboats had washed ashore near Madeira. All hope had evaporated when she turned up after prolonging her voyage to avoid submarines in the area.

Another son, Albert Wynne, was badly gassed serving in the army on the Western Front. When he returned home a pivoting summerhouse was built for him in the garden at Auckland House. According to Molly Williams, his niece, he would spend most of his days in there lying on a horsehair couch, with family members sporadically rotating the construction to ensure maximum sunlight. It was eventually decided for his health's sake, that he go and live in South Africa, and it was there that he died in 1933.

Lewis and Anne's third son Lewis (1845–1937) began his career as ship's boy on the schooner *Mary Jane*. Later he gained his master's certificate in 1870, and commanded a series of sailing ships, the *Martha Lloyd* for seven years and the *Naomi* for another seven (until she was lost in 1882), the *Granville, Claudia, Coromandel* and the *Caradog*. He is reputed to have rounded Cape Horn more times than any other captain from Borth, apparently some fourteen times.

The fourth son David (1849–1910), mentioned earlier, gained his master mariners certificate at Dublin in 1874. To celebrate this occasion he bought himself a gold watch. During his career, he had to apply twice for replacement master's certificates that were lost in the sinkings of the barques *General Nott* and the *Inchbarga*. In 1892, the *General Nott* was lost after a collision with a French ship in the English Channel. David and his brother John, had shares in her. Three years later another certificate was applied for when the *Inchbarga* sank in the Black Sea. In a thirty-year career he also commanded the sailing barques *Ivanhoe, Earl Cadogan* and the *Glenholm*. Captain Williams died on the *Glenholm* at Hull, and is buried in Llandre church cemetery.

David married Mary Jane, a widow who was from the seafaring Jones family of Ffosygravel. Mary Jane's first husband, Captain Evan Hughes (1849–82) had died at sea of liver disease shortly after they were married and there were no children from this union. Evan Hughes became captain in 1855, and commanded the *Hannah* (1874–77), *Hugh Ewing* (1877–79) and *Spirit of the South* (1879–82). David and Mary Jane had two children, but only Elsie survived as her brother Edgar died at four years old. Soon afterwards, tragedy struck again as Mary Jane died whilst her husband was away at sea. Captain David Williams then married Ann Jones, his deceased wife's first cousin, and daughter of Thomas and Elizabeth Jones of Ffosygravel. This second union produced a daughter Anna, and she and her half sister Elsie attended primary school at nearby Llandre. Later the two girls went together to the Welsh Girls' School at Ashford in Middlesex.

Elsie sailed to India in 1916 on the *City of York*, the last ship on which women and children were allowed to travel after the start of World War One, to marry Jenkin Jones Hughes, a curate working for the Cambridge Mission to Delhi. Three years later in 1919, the couple returned to find Elsie's half-sister Anna dying. Elsie's only daughter, named Anna in memory of her aunt, married Robert Heathcote and they had two children, Diana and Tony, who provided the images of the barques *Glenholm* and the *Earl Cadogan*.

Captain David Williams' gold watch had narrow escape: when the *Inchbarga* sank after the collision in the Black Sea, Captain Williams, after taking to the boats, realised the watch was still aboard. After a mad scramble, he retrieved it just in time from his already waterlogged cabin. After his death in 1910, the watch was given to his son-in-law Jenkin Jones Hughes. In his duties as a curate, he always had it on a shelf near the pulpit so that he could time his sermons.

Captain David Williams commanded the barque *Earl Cadogan*, from 1896 to 1899. Amongst many destinations were Ascension, St. Helena, Natal, Algoa Bay, the east coast and Gulf ports of the USA, Burma, Mauritius and the Red Sea, then the barque *Glenholm* (1902–1909), voyaging to Brazil, River Plate, Australia, New Zealand, Ascension, Natal, South Pacific and the west coast of America.

The other sons of Lewis and Anne, namely Thomas and Richard, were also mariners, but very little information is available about them, except that they both died young. Thomas (b. 1847) was named after his dead sibling and is believed to have died overseas in South America. Richard (1852–73) is buried at Llandre churchyard.

The previously mentioned barque *Aberystwyth Castle* was built in 1875 by R. G. Evans & Co, Liverpool. Her first owners were the Welsh Castle Line, but twenty years later she ended up in the hands of Australian owners. Luckily a fine picture of this iron-hulled barque survives; it was painted in Newcastle, New South Wales. After a long association with Borth mariners, she ended her days in the Pacific; she was badly damaged off Japan in a typhoon in 1900 and broken up.

When this ship was commanded by Captain William Williams, the first mate was often Hugh Hughes (1827–1901), although having gained his master's certificate in 1869, he was first mate on the *Aberystwyth Castle* from 1876 to 1882. He later captained the barque *Rhuddlan Castle*, but his master's certificate was suspended after the vessel became stranded on the Goodwin Sands. He continued at sea only as first officer on the *Primrose Castle*, but he and all the crew except one drowned when she foundered off Holyhead in 1901.

Captain William Williams (b. 1839) had three mariner sons: John (1864–1907), Lewis (1868–1952) and David (1873-94). All three had sailed with their father and their two uncles in many of the previously-listed sailing ships. John became captain in 1890 and commanded the *Clarissa Radcliffe*, and later the *Orianda* (1904–1907). He and his wife Elizabeth lived at Deudraeth. He drowned when the *Orianda* was involved in a collision off Nash Point in the Bristol Channel in February 1907, on a voyage from Cardiff to Spezia, Italy.

Lewis Williams was second mate in 1891, first mate in 1893 and captain in 1896. Amongst the vessels he commanded were the steamships *Vindomora* (1898), *Porthcawl* (1904–1909), *Castle Bruce* (1914–1917), the *Foreric* (1918) and the *Carston* (1920). Captain Lewis Williams married Lizzie Hughes (1869–1946), of Rhyd Y Cerrig Cottage. Her sister, Sarah Hughes, married Captain John Jones, and they had a son, Horace Ivor Jones, who became a ship's captain. A descendant, Myra Noreen Ford, nee Williams, has a treasured possession from her great aunt, Sarah Jones, nee Hughes, in the form of a gold brooch, brought back, no doubt, from a sea voyage. It consists of three solid gold Deutschmarks, dated 1878, one of which was struck at Hamburg.

David, about whom we have little information, died in Rio de Janeiro at twenty-one years old. Prior to 1920, the Williams family lived opposite the Friendship Inn, in Picton House, which later became Arfor. When the family moved to the row of large houses at the northern end of the village, they took the name Picton with them.

When Captain Lewis Williams' only son Llewelyn Vernon (1897–1980) was a young boy his father would send postcards home from all around the world. Most were to his wife Lizzie, but many were to the young son, saying such as 'Hope you are keeping a very good boy and that you will be coming for a voyage soon…' in 1905 when he was eight years old; 'Are you ready to come away with me?…', when Vernon was nine; 'A little bird has been telling me that you have been smoking cigarettes, all right my boy you wait till I get home. I hope that you won't do it again and be a good boy…', this when he was twelve years old. It is obvious that there was a deep affection between father and son, which lasted a lifetime; probably strengthened later on when Vernon's sister Noreen (1895–1928) died of tuberculosis whilst both father and son were away at sea. However, her name lived on, as relatives David and May Hughes of Boston House asked if they could name their daughter after her. This they did, and until her recent death, Noreen Sharpe lived in Borth at West End, where her daughter and family currently live.

Throughout the First World War, Vernon sailed with his father as first mate, without mishap. 'Vernon Bach', as he was affectionately known, was constantly up to mischief, and refused to take life too seriously. The stories about him are many. Even when he sailed with his father he could not resist getting involved in all sorts of escapades despite having the responsibility of being first mate. On one occasion just before Christmas, Vernon and his Borth shipmates stole a couple of sacks of walnuts from a warehouse in Marseilles. The gendarmes narrowed the suspects down, and came to search the ship, but to no avail. However, his father Captain Lewis Williams discovered where the nuts had been hidden, and gathered his son and cohorts together and told them that the price for his silence was one of the sacks … half the loot! Gales of laughter burst out and they readily agreed, as they did not want to spend the festive season in a French jail. No doubt, the sound of walnuts being cracked at Picton resonated throughout the house that particular Christmas, whilst father and son exchanged a wink.

Vernon studied for his second and first mate tickets at Cardiff Maritime College. He also passed his master's mariner's examination; unfortunately, it was discovered that he was colour-blind, so he was excluded from commanding vessels.

He married Elizabeth Ann David (1905–1979), who was also from a seafaring family from south Ceredigion. Two of her uncles were sea captains: one, from Newcastle Emlyn, commanded the *SS Bretwalda* throughout the First World War. Borth man Evan John Rees of Gordon Villa, ship's cook and the son of Captain Hugh Rees, survived the torpedoing of the *SS Bretwalda* near Malta in 1917. Elizabeth Ann's other uncle, having moved to Portsmouth also served as captain in the same conflict on the *SS Empress of Britain*, which

The Jones Family (Craiglea)

Vernon's cousin, Horace Ivor Jones 1895–1963, first went to sea at sixteen years old with his uncle Captain Lewis, Williams Picton House, on the *Castle Bruce*. Vernon and Horace were popular characters who were constantly getting into mischief. At one time, they caused a great stir in the village by firing shots from revolvers that each had brought back from sea. There was a great hullabaloo but no one was hurt or prosecuted.

Guns and the Williams family were no strangers. At the wedding of Vernon's great uncle Captain Lewis Williams to the daughter of local butcher Evan Hughes, it was reported that 'at an early hour guns were fired and flags were flying at various places out of respect for the young couple'.

Horace Jones lived at his family home, Craiglea, and went to sea in 1910. He was on the steamships *Lady Carrington, Armenia* and *Saracen*, before becoming third mate in 1915 on the *SS Menapeam*. His next vessels were the steamers *Usher, Broompark, Slav* and *Southern*. He became second mate in 1921 on the steamships *Elmpark* and *H. H. Asquith*, and got his master's certificate in 1928. Subsequently he served as first mate on many vessels, including, *Backworth, Knight of Saint John, Knight of the Realm* and *Cape Howe*. By 1937, he gained his first command, the *Cape Sable*. his wife joined him on board on several occasions. All this came to an abrupt end with the Second World War, as the *Cape Sable*, with Captain H. I. Jones, now seconded into the RNR with the rank of Lieutenant Commander, saw some of the grimmer aspects of the conflict, especially in the Baltic Sea. Horace was also related to the Jones mariners of Maesarfor.

The Ellis Family

When shoemaker John Ellis (b. 1853), from an old Machynlleth family going back to a Hugh Ellis in the 1700s, married Borth girl Mary James, it was the beginning of another dynasty in the maritime history of Borth. Mary came from an illustrious family which had produced master mariners for generations. John and Mary were to have three sons, all of whom had connections with the sea, starting with Captain David Ellis (1880–1961), John Hayden Ellis (1886–1940), and Rowland Hugh Ellis (1894–1960).

David Ellis became second mate in 1903, first mate in 1905, and passed as master in 1908. He was captain of the *Mexico, Glenavy, Lantaro, Lobos* and the *Losada*; the *Salvador* was his last command in 1938. He retired to Llys Iago in Penybont after his seafaring days.

John Hayden Ellis, as a young merchant mariner, went to live in Freemantle, West Australia, for a few years before the First World War. It was there that he married Annie, who had emigrated there in 1911 from London on the *SS Otranto*. Their first son, John (Jac) David Ellis, was born in 1917. Whilst Hayden Ellis was in Australia, he was awarded a Royal Humane Society of Australia Certificate of Merit, which reads as follows:

> It was resolved that the courage and humanity displayed by John Hayden Ellis of the Pilot Station, Albany, W.A., boatman, aged 27 years, who risked his life in attempting to rescue William Thomas West from drowning at Albany on November 9th 1913 … entitles him to the Certificate of Merit of this society'.

Part of the citation is as follows:

> West fell off the jetty into the sea, which was very rough and the tide running out. Ellis ran a quarter of a mile and went out in a boat to the rescue. He then dived into 16 feet of water, and reached West. He bought him to the jetty, but all efforts at resuscitation failed'.

The Humane Society of Australia published a book in 1994 called '7,000 Brave Australians', which included the Ellis rescue. Recently John Hayden's grandson John wryly observed 'Perhaps the title should be amended to '6,999 Brave Australians and a Mariner from Borth'. The family returned to Britain on the SS *Orsova* and moved back to Borth to live at White Lion House, today's Beatrice, where another son, Thomas Ellis, was born in 1920.

Australian-born Jac attended Morfa School, and was happily continuing his studies at the age of fourteen when things suddenly changed for him. He remembers his father coming back from sea, and having an unusually long series of whispered discussions with his mother, which were quite mystifying. The next thing he knew his parents returned from Aberystwyth with a pair of overalls which he was told to try on. After a successful fitting, with room to grow, he was informed that he was going to sea with his father, who was bosun on the SS *Earlspark*. On his first voyage to Newfoundland Jac remembers being violently seasick.

Father and son sailed together on this vessel for the next five years, visiting many small ports on the east and west coasts of Africa. On one occasion, when he was sixteen, he remembers being a little bit tense and a touch annoyed when he found himself at the wheel, fast approaching Durban, and expecting any minute to be relieved by a more experienced seaman. This did not happen; he was told in no uncertain terms that not only had he done well, but that very few sixteen-year-olds would have been allowed such a privilege.

In 1938 Jac was footloose in Borth doing some painting and decorating with his pal Enoch Pugh of the Friendship Inn. Seeking further adventure, he decided one day to go to the Drill Hall in Aberystwyth and join the army. He served in the Welsh Guards throughout the Second World War, and was part of the British Expeditionary Force that escaped from Dunkirk. He later went back to Europe as part of the Liberation Army. Unbeknown to him, he was to be in the contingent that liberated a prisoner-of-war camp that young Borth seaman Harry Jones had been held in since 1939. As Jac recalls, it was only at the end of the war, when he was back home, that he realized Harry had been at that particular camp. Jac's war was spent in the dangerous duties of petrol lorry driver, constantly re-supplying the tanks along the front line. Jac recalls that he often slept under the truck, which would have been lethal if it had got hit.

After the war, he was offered work as a painter and decorator in the Midlands, where he stayed. He is now retired and living at Great Barr, Birmingham. Another ex-seaman Edwin Jenkins, of Otago House, who had served in the Royal Navy during the Second World War, also moved away to become a painter and decorator in Llanidloes.

Jac's father, John Hayden Ellis, was not so lucky. He had continued to serve as bosun on the 5,250 ton *SS Earlspark*. This vessel was torpedoed in 1940 by a U101 whilst on a voyage from Sunderland with a cargo of coal bound for France, approximately 60 nautical miles northwest of Cape Finisterre. The captain at the time of this tragedy was Evan James Williams of Borth. According to the thirty-one survivors, John Hayden Ellis again displayed selfless courage by desperately trying to save the captain, and in this process lost his own life.

Rowland Hugh Ellis was at sea most of his life, and served as bosun on the *Pontwern Oakfield, Zeelandier, Beechpark, Wheatsheaf, Penhill, Welsh City, Leeds City* and the *New Westminster City*. In 1916, he was torpedoed on the *Margam Abbey*, and in January of the following year, he survived the torpedoing of the *Lady Carrington*. No sooner was he home from the latter event than he was off to Barry to join another ship! In 1918, with Captain Williams of Picton House, in command of the *SS Foreric*, Rowland, who lived in Carron House, joined the Borth crew contingent consisting of Vernon Williams Picton, John Davies Trigfan and Gwilym Davies Nathaniel, at Borth railway station to travel to Glasgow to join the ship. Later in 1934 Rowland survived the wrecking of the *Plas Dinam* which ran aground in dense fog off the coast of Newfoundland.

Jac Ellis was great friends with the Pugh boys of the Friendship Inn. Freddy was in the RAF, Enoch in the Royal Marines and Jacky was in the Royal navy in the 1930s serving on *HMS Rodney* and *HMS Despatch* after training at HMS Ganges Harwich.

Mishaps at sea were experienced by most mariners, some of whom were at sea until their 70s, such as William Jones (1847–1918), who was seventy-one when he lost his life after a torpedo attack on the *SS Rysdael*. Archibald Morgan Rees (b. 1857) was second mate on the *Kelvinside* in 1887, when she foundered at Mauritius. Later at sixty-one years old, he survived the torpedoing of the *SS Bernard* at the end of World War One.

The Davies Family (Wesleyan Place)

The Davies clan of fisherfolk were to become enmeshed in another tragic outcome of the First World War. Some of the family appear in a fabulous photograph taken by either the local chemist, Mr. Williams, or Dr Herbert Beadnell. The latter wrote a book, published in 1920, grandly titled *An Extraordinary Guide to the City of Borth*, in which he lauds the lobster-catching prowess of one family member, Richard Davies (1863–1917). Within a few years of the photograph being taken around 1912, three of the four men appearing in it had died in tragic circumstances.

By 1916 Royal Naval Reservist Richard Davies was already a veteran who had been awarded good conduct and long service medals. In 1915, he had been praised for his part in the attempted salvage of the 2000-ton steamer *Van Stirum*. This vessel had been attacked just off Liverpool by two German submarines. After trying to desperately dodge them, the captain decided, for the safety of his crew, to take to the boats, abandoning the stricken vessel.

Richard Davies, who at the time was on a patrol vessel, volunteered with three others to take a boat and board the still-floating steamer and try to tie a line to her. The boarding party managed to get to her just as their own boat smashed itself against the steamer's side. They managed to fix a towing hawser to her, but she started listing alarmingly. Thankfully, their patrol boat skipper realized the danger they were in and got them off just in time before the *Van Stirum* turned turtle and sank. On 25 March 1917, Richard Davies died while serving on the *Evangel*, off Milford Haven, which had been engaged in mine-sweeping operations. He left a widow, Mary, and six children: David, Thomas, Jane, Mary, John and Richard. At the time, son Richard was on active service with the Royal Welch Fusiliers and John in the Royal Navy, serving on *HMS Caesar* and *HMS Pomone*.

James Davies, the older brother of Richard, was also a Royal Naval Reservist. He served on the *HMS Ocean* and the *HMS King*

Alfred on mine-sweeping duties, but had been retired as he had lost the sight of one eye on active service. Within seven months of his brother Richard's death, he too died.

Events in 1917, far from the home waters of Maes Gwyddno, triggered James' fate. The 6,305-ton *SS Memphian*, of Liverpool, was on her way to New Orleans when she was torpedoed eight miles east of the Arklow lightship with the loss of thirty-two crew-members. This vessel had already entered history as having warned the ill-fated *Titanic* about icebergs.

By the end of the week, the wreckage from the stricken *Memphian* reached northern Ceredigion waters. The flotsam, which included oars and hatch covers marked *Memphian*, was strewn from Traeth Bach at Wallog to Trwyn Pellaf, and two bodies were washed ashore at Borth beach. Part of the ship's cargo of cork bales was also found in the vicinity and were valuable enough to warrant being salvaged.

James Davies and his nephew David (1895–1917) were joined by thirteen-year-old Harry Jones of Troedyrhiw as they prepared to set out from Borth beach in the family boat. Four-year-old Jac Richards of Maelgwyn was one of the last to see them alive early that Thursday morning, and recalled just being able to see out of a downstairs window, watching the preparations of the boating party prior to leaving the beach. He said, 'It was very misty and sometimes they vanished and reappeared as the mist periodically cleared. I saw them row out a little way then they totally disappeared.' Their purpose was to salvage the many floating bales of cork. In all probability all three fell into the water and drowned after capsizing their boat whilst attempting to roll the large cork bales into it.

By 3 o'clock on the same day, Harry Jones' mother became alarmed at the deteriorating weather conditions combined with Harry's late return. Passing Pengoitan she walked up towards Craig Y Wylfa, but before getting there she saw the upside down boat drifting off Trwyn Canol, which was later recovered on the Aberdyfi bar on Friday morning. There was no sign of the men. The womenfolk of the Davies family, accompanied by Harry Jones' parents, kept vigil on Craig Y Wylfa for weeks on end, but the bodies were never recovered.

A sequel to these events took place in 1921 when the Borth War

Memorial Committee decided to omit the name of James Davies, RNR, Wesleyan Place, from the war memorial, because officially he had been invalided out of the service prior to his death. However, the villagers immediately drew up a successful petition to ensure that his name was not be erased, and furthermore that the other two drowned salvagers were to be included .

The only male survivor of those appearing in the photograph mentioned above was John James Davies, or as he was known locally, Jac Shami. He joined the Royal Navy and served on *HMS Hood*. Later, like his cousin John William Davies, he continued sailing as a merchant seaman, and he appears in photographs from the 1930s on the *Cape Howe, Stanholm* and *Dallas City.*

John William Davies (b. 1893) was a seaman all his life. After serving with distinction in the Royal Navy in the First World War, he joined the Merchant Navy. He was on the *Cape Howe* and then served on several Port Line vessels. In December of 1938, whilst serving on the *MV Dallas City*, he was hospitalized in Korea suffering from pneumonia, from which he died. Evan William Lewis of Panteg was on the same ship; he was to lose his life two years later in 1940, when the *SS Bradfyne* was torpedoed. Amongst the mourners at John's funeral in Korea were the captains and crew of the *Dallas City, Fresno City* and *SS Llangollen*. John William Davies often sailed with Borth relatives and friends, as some fine photographs attest.

This Borth fisher-family had done their duty in time of war, often paying with their lives, and their descendants continue to produce mariners and man local lifeboats, with Borth's Ronnie Davies being awarded the MBE for his services to the RNLI.

Other Borth relatives were Evan Davies, Mona House, and his son Evan Leslie. Captain Evan Leslie Davies was awarded an OBE for services rendered during the Second World War. His vessel was attacked many times from the air, by E-Boat and long-range guns. His defensive strategies were highly praised, and it was noted that he showed consistent courage, skill and seamanship. It is curious to think that during the Depression in the 1930s this talented mariner was for a time forced to find work on land in the police force.

The Davies family can be traced back to the 1700s, with an Evan Davies (b. 1796) marrying an Ann (b. 1806) at Borth. Evan is a Christian name that persists down the generations in the

Aberystwyth branch of the family. Some Davies fishermen moved to Aberystwyth around the 1850s and took the beach-fisher tradition of their native village with them, and also took the Borth-designed beach boat. For generations they supplied coxswains and crew for the Aberystwyth Lifeboat. One of the Davies women married into the Parry family of Trefechan, and gave their offspring a saltwater perspective, with many Parrys becoming major players in Aberystwyth-based fisheries.

A descendant of the Davies family that went to Aberystwyth, Evan Desmond Davies (b. 1924), related that his grandfather Evan, and his great-uncle, John, moved their families and furniture from Borth to Aberystwyth by sea. These brothers were a fiery pair and in one dispute over ownership of a small boat, Evan resolved matters by taking a hand saw, going down to Aberystwyth harbour and cutting it in half.

The brothers owned two large sailing trawlers, the *Gypsy King* and the *Gypsy Maid*. The former sailed to Borth, anchored offshore and sent a punt on to the beach to transfer both families' household items onto the larger vessel, and sailed south to Aberystwyth. There is a fine Alfred Worthington painting of the *Gypsy King*, depicting her with some of her sails torn, as this was how she returned after one

Desmond Davies' family on the Gypsy King, one of their sailing trawlers

memorable five-day fishing trip, just prior to the artist painting her. She was a beam trawler, with only one mechanical device aboard, a steam winch, for hauling the net aboard.

Desmond often wondered how his grandfather Evan met and married a girl from Welshpool. The answer was simple: she was the daughter of the Simister family of rope-makers that the brothers did business with. Apparently, this formidable lady was the business brain of the family, and when she died she left a substantial portfolio of Aberystwyth properties. According to Desmond, his grandfather needed somebody to tighten the rein, as after his fishing trips his wife would limit his access to the profit as he was prone to overindulge in the local pubs. To compensate for this enforced lack of funds Evan would apparently tap dance on an inverted dinner plate in the pub to entertain patrons who would show their appreciation by buying him drinks.

At a glance, the mariners in direct descent from Evan (b. 1796), are Evan (b. 1837), a master mariner who by 1881 was living in Aberystwyth; Evan (b. 1859), who was mate on the *Picton Castle*; and Evan James (b. 1898), who served on the *Lusitania* and the *Mauritania*, as well as being in the RNR during World War One. He received a Russian Medal in 1916 for participating in the rescue of a Russian family whilst serving on *HMS Jupiter*.

Evan Desmond Davies went to sea on the *Lottie R* with Captain John Brodigan, a relative of the Williams and Brodigan families of Borth. Desmond served through the latter years of the Second World War, then left the sea for a time, re-joined when he was fifty in 1974, and stayed on until he was sixty-five. As he maintains, there were huge changes between his two periods at sea. One of his sons, Evan John Davies, was a mariner for fourteen years.

The Jones Family
(Troedyrhiw and Panteg)

The previously mentioned Jones family of Troedyrhiw, whose son Harry drowned whilst salvaging with the Davies men, were soon to lose another son to tuberculosis. Two other sons were in the army at the time and a third, Thomas, was at sea on the same ship as my grandfather. By 1917, Thomas had joined the RNR and served on *HMS Drake*. In 1930, two of the sons jumped ship in Australia, and were, for a time, looked after by a young couple who had gone from Borth to Melbourne as teachers. Gwen Lloyd, who lives next door at Frondirion, is still mystified sixty years later as to why their parents did not send money for a passage home, despite the Jones' running a successful market garden enterprise at Troedyrhiw.

Harry Jones' name lived on in another seafaring relative, David Henry 'Harry' Jones (1924–1981) of Panteg House. Harry joined the Merchant Navy in 1939 and his first voyage ended abruptly when his ship was impounded in Hamburg after World War Two was declared. The crew were force-marched through wintry conditions to a German prisoner-of-war camp, where he remained for the duration. At the camp he befriended another prisoner, Chief Steward John Stanley Hampson (1919-71).

Harry had no idea that during his internment that his father had died, nor that two of his sisters, Lilian and Mary, were in the Womens Royal Army Corps. Lilian served in Malaysia and Mary in Europe. At the war's end, prior to their repatriation to Britain, Harry and John were at a huge celebratory party held in an aeroplane hangar. Whilst Harry was dancing, he literally bumped into his WRAC sister Mary. John was introduced to her and romance immediately blossomed, and after returning to Britain, they married and lived at Borth. After nearly a decade, John returned to sea, sailing from Newport on the *Welsh Minstrel*. I clearly remember him going and returning from his voyages, always carrying a small old-fashioned leather suitcase.

Harry returned to sea with the Manchester Lines, at the cessation of hostilities. He frequently travelled to America and Canada on the *Manchester Commerce* and *Manchester Port,* visiting many ports including Chicago. He was a character that loomed large in my youth as every time he came back from sea it was party time, both in the village pubs and in the now-vanished Panteg, where his widowed mother and his sisters and their families would have roaring good times.

I met him several times in Sydney where I would join him on the *Asian Renown,* another vessel run by Manchester Lines. Harry served this company as a bosun for thirty years. He took his wife Anne with him on several voyages. Sadly, he died of cancer in 1981. One of his pals, who lived across the lane in front of his house, was Ronald Jenkins who was in the Royal Navy during the Second World War. When they were home from sea at the same time they would often rig up a breeches buoy from the upper floors of their respective homes, causing great consternation amongst users of the laneway they 'crossed over'. Ronald was quite a character. After returning to Borth at the end of the war, he, like a few others, decided to move away and seek employment elsewhere.

Another of Harry Jones' brothers-in-law, Idris Wyn Jones (b. 1928), was at sea for over sixteen years, from 1944–60. He served on sixty ships belonging mainly to the Blue Funnel Line. Amongst the vessels he was on were the *Agapenor, Laomedo, Mentor, Cyclops, Stentor, Jason, Demodocus* and the *Rhesus.* In the final year of the Second World War he was in the Far East carrying ammunition and supplies to Surabaya, Batavia and Port Moresby. After the end of hostilities the ships he was on were returning supplies and vehicles to Australia, and he often voyaged to Japan around this time.

The Herbert Family

I can think of no better way to introduce the next Borth character than to relate the following tale. On a fine carnival day, around 1960, a few friends and I gathered at the old bus shelter opposite the then Canteen Stores, now the Nisa Store, to witness the arrival of carnival participants. The procedure in those days was that participants gathered at the southern end of the village and paraded northwards through the village to end at Pantyfedwen, where they gathered on its steps for a group photograph. As carnival entrants streamed towards the starting point, there was suddenly a loud pistol shot and a clattering of hooves coming from the back lane near the now vanished Panteg. Out came a white horse, on which rode a highwayman dressed in green silk livery, three-cornered hat and black riding boots. After a startled moment or two we realized that it was Captain Herbert. In the general hubbub, the horse reared and from the crowd emerged the village policeman, Sergeant Rees, who grabbed the reins. Strong words were exchanged in Welsh concerning safety and horsemanship, but the captain reclaimed the reins, and gave the sergeant short shrift. After all, no mere village 'bobby' was going to admonish a man who had captained ships and men in many a perilous situation

Captain Lewis James Herbert, who was at sea from 1917 to 1955

for over forty years. With another defiant pistol shot, horse and rider galloped away from the throng northward to Y Graig, where in a cascade of hoof sparks, the highwayman turned his steed around and came to a halt by the entrance to Gerydon, where the captain's two spinster sisters gazed in adoration from the bay window at their wag of a brother. We were left guffawing at the obviously embarrassed and fuming policeman. The captain had made our day.

As a child, Lewis James Herbert attended Morfa Primary School, essentially for the children of church-going families. He was then sent, when sturdy enough to do so, to walk the distance to Top School, which was for chapelgoers. Later he was sent as a boarder to Towyn County School.

L. J. Herbert's first voyage began on 10 May 1917 under the watchful eye of his uncle Captain J. O. Enos. This was on the *SS Cheltonian* of Cardiff, where he shared a cabin with fellow-villager and second mate Henry Levi Williams. This first voyage only lasted twenty-nine days as shelling from a U- boat sank the ship. The crew took to the life-boats. Fortunately they were only fifty miles from land, which they reached fifteen hours later, close to Marseilles. The master, Captain Enos, and one of the gunners were taken prisoner. Lewis James lost all his possessions, and arrived home a week or so later to re-equip himself. Despite parental pleading for him to return to school, he instead befriended Captain Lewis, Glan-y-don House, and went on three trips with him on a coaster. He persisted in going to sea and was on the *SS Merioneth* in the summer of 1924 as an AB. His father, Captain John Herbert, realizing that he was going to pursue a career at sea come what may; decided that he should have a proper apprenticeship. Captain John Herbert had married Margarita Enos, daughter of Captain J. O. Enos, and the couple lived at Gerydon. In 1900, as Second Officer on the *SS Hilary*, he showed outstanding courage in effecting the rescue of the captain and crew of the American schooner *Mary E. Lermond*. For his efforts he received a Presidential Medal.

During his apprenticeship L. J. Herbert served on the *Southern, Utah* and the *Middlemor*. Another of the Enos family, Idwal O. Enos, commanded the *Southern*. Most of the officers and crew came from Borth and Aberystwyth. From his home village were David Enos,

John William Davies, Horace Jones, Emlyn Herbert, R. R. Davies and Gwilym Davies.

Back at Borth it was time to settle down to study for examinations. Eventually he obtained his first mate's ticket, and took a berth as chief officer on the smallest ship he was ever to serve on. This vessel, the *Myrtis*, had to steam across the Atlantic to Canada. Her master and owner was Captain John Davies of Maesteg, Borth. Among her crew were another two locals, Leslie Davies of Mona House, and Alan Jones, the local electrician.

L. J. Herbert decided to sit for his master's ticket at Halifax Nova Scotia, and six weeks after obtaining his ticket he assumed command of the *Myrtis*. This vessel traded between the Eastern Ports of Canada and the Great Lakes. On one occasion winter set in early. The ship became trapped in the ice, and explosives had to be used to free her. After serving four years on the vessel he decided it was time to return home. He went to Cardiff to see what employment prospects there were. Unexpectedly he was immediately offered a berth as chief officer. He agreed to accept the position on one condition, which took the ship-owner by surprise, as it seemed a little impertinent: he explained that he had been overseas in Canada for four years and desperately wanted to see his fiancée Meriona Ellis Davies at Borth. Thankfully, the owner knew the girl and agreed to this immediately. Later, when the couple got married, the owner came to the wedding and stayed in Borth for a week. From that time on he was continually employed as a master.

The Spanish Civil War was by this time at its height, and soon he was instructed to run the blockade to Spanish Ports. His ship, *Candleston Castle*, was sent to St. Jean de Luz in South West France, to await orders. Thoroughly enamoured with this delightful port, he named his first daughter Jean after it. Orders came to proceed to Santander where he arrived without sighting any of General Franco's warships. The cargo was discharged – albeit under difficult conditions as Franco's aeroplanes were sporadically dropping bombs. The vessel was then loaded with refugees to be taken to France. Suddenly a serious air raid began, by which time there were 2,400 refugees on board the *Candleston Castle*, ranging in age from ninety years old to babes in arms. The quayside was deserted except for a lone Briton who 'let go' the lines. Captain Herbert turned to speak to the Pilot, who had evidently thought that discretion was the better part of valour and had already jumped ashore to take shelter during the raid. When the raid was over, the ship left port safely.

Soon some of the male refugees, having spotted one of Franco's cruisers, went to the lower bridge to hand over their revolvers just in case the ship was searched, because those found with arms were at risk of being shot. When the ship reached the three-mile limit a British destroyer came alongside and asked if there were any men of military age on board. After giving the destroyer's Commander a negative answer, Captain Herbert decided to get everyone below deck quickly. Franco's cruiser came over to inspect, but a British destroyer intervened and they were allowed to proceed on their way, and sailed without incident to Bordeaux. The vessel arrived in Bordeaux with 2,402 refugees, which led to much bickering because the manifest showed only 2,400. The reason for this was that two children had been born at sea between Spain and France. One of Captain Herbert's most nostalgic memories was the rousing cheer these refugees gave the ship's company as their train steamed out of the Bordeaux Quayside.

On a mission to pick up more refugees the ship was captured and escorted to Ferrol and had to stay therefor the next two months. The crew were treated very well, but not allowed to leave the ship. Letters took four days to come from home. Captain Herbert contemplated raising steam and running out of port at night. Fortunately he had second thoughts because when they were allowed to go they found that the entrance had been substantially mined! While captive in the port, being a true 'Cardi' the captain rented out the ship's tarpaulins to Franco's men so that they could cover their dockside ammunition stocks. After returning to Cardiff, the crew was complemented on being one of the cleanest ships to come into port. No doubt that the two months in Ferrol without shore-leave had a lot to do with this! After being given forty-eight hours leave to see his newborn baby daughter, Captain Herbert returned again to Spain, this time under different circumstances: the Franco regime had chartered his ship!

Then a much bigger war broke out in Europe. World War Two brought its perils on two occasions. The first was when the captain was bombed on entering the Thames in 1940. The explosion shattered all the instruments on board including the compasses. It was always a source of amazement to him how the German plane managed to find them, when at that time the visibility was down to 100 yards. The vessel was escorted to Harwich and when asked the time of the incident the evidence was there aplenty: all the clocks had stopped at 11 a.m.

The second time was in the South Atlantic, when the *Elmwood* was bound from New York to the Persian Gulf – via the Cape of Good Hope, with a general cargo. On 27 July 1942, it was torpedoed, and for Captain Herbert it was a sad thing that a ship, which was only two months and twenty-two days old, should be destroyed. Eleven days and 6½ hours later the captain sailed his lifeboat into Freetown Harbour. There were thirteen crew-members in the lifeboat, including Captain Herbert, with one engineer apparently unable to walk at this time. The Chief Officer's boat was picked up five days later by an American ship; the Second Officer's boat landed on an island 200 miles north of Freetown the same day that Captain Herbert's boat landed. The captain arrived home early in September with his weight down to 7 stone. The ship owners kept him home for nine months before allowing him to sail again.

Other ships that Captain Lewis James Herbert served on as an officer in the next eleven years were SS *Whinefield*, *Seven Seas Transport* (ex *Picton*), *David Lloyd George*, *Myrtis*, *Ulva*, *Seven Seas Sound*, *Greenmuir* and *Glenwood*. His last command was the *Catrine*, a 5,219-ton vessel belonging to the Morell Line, which voyaged to Australia and New Zealand. He continued at sea until 1955 as master, and eventually when home on leave from one ship, visited his doctor for a check-up and was advised to call it a day as he was suffering from a nervous complaint, so it was then that he 'swallowed the anchor'.

He lived a life straight out of the pages of Boys Own; he was quirky and kind, but he never suffered fools gladly. I am sure that he would approve of my closing his story by relating an incident that happened after repatriation to Britain folowing the sinking of the *Elmwood* in 1942. Having arrived back in Scotland from South Africa, he boarded the night train south to Borth. He summoned the attendant and asked for a cup of tea. The unwise reply from the unwitting steward was, 'Don't you know there is a bloody war on?' Captain Herbert, in Welsh and English, ensured that the attendant and several others in the vicinity would never forget the withering reply.

He literally left this world with a bang. Arrangements had been made for the Borth lifeboat to take his ashes out to sea opposite the village. In a final salute rockets were fired from the shore, but unfortunately no-one had informed the authorities. The next thing sirens were heard wailing from ambulance and police vehicles. When all was explained, Sergeant John the local policeman, said with a wry smile, 'I could have guessed it was Captain Herbert causing a riot to the end'.

As he had two daughters the maritime tradition jumped a generation and resumed with his grandson Peter John Caswell, son of Ken and Jean, who joined the Blue Star Line and became a ship's engineer. He served on the *Mahsuri, Columbia Star, Act 1, Act 5, Act 7, Wellington Star* and the *Southern Star*. He was also on the *Keren*, an ex-North Sea ferry chartered by the Ministry of Defence to carry troops to the Falklands. On his last voyage from San Francisco and New Zealand the shipping company folded and the vessel was flagged out whilst they were at Fiji. This was only a matter of months before Peter was to become chief engineer. As his father Ken relates, 'I went to meet a very unhappy son, but noticed that he clutched a parcel in his hand which he triumphantly revealed to contain the Red Duster that he had taken from his last vessel.' Peter is currently a consultant engineer on terra firma.

John Emlyn Herbert, Lewis James' older brother, born in 1899, also went to sea. However, his naval career began with a hiccup as his parents had to fetch him home from Liverpool in October 1916, as he had contracted typhoid fever. By 1934 he was first officer on the *Plas Dinam* when she was wrecked off the Newfoundland coast.

John Emlyn moved to live in Cardiff and went on to become a master mariner with an illustrious career at sea that ended when he lost his life while serving as captain of the small 600 ton coaster *Dungrange*. This vessel was named *Okehampton* in 1925, *Yewbank* in 1926 and *Dungrange* in 1937, when Buchan and Hogg of Grangemouth owned it. In June 1944 Captain J. E. Herbert was taking a cargo of provisions, ammunition and fuel from the Isle of Wight to the Normandy beaches as part of a convoy of twenty ships. He was on his third trip when an E-boat off St Catherine's Point attacked the vessel. The *Dungrange* had gone to the aid of the *Brackensfield*, which had been attacked and sunk. In the act of searching for survivors, two other E-boats appeared and sank the *Dungrange* with torpedoes. Eighteen crew-members perished, including Captain J. E. Herbert.

John Emlyn had already seen action in 1940 when as captain of the *Sarastone* (mentioned earlier in a Borth context), successfully fought off a surface U-boat attack off the coast of Portugal on a passage back to the UK. There were other incidents during World War Two. John Emlyn was in command of the *SS Wild Rose* when she was bombed by German aircraft off the coast of Ireland. Badly damaged, she was towed in to Rosslare Harbour by the *MV Kericgue*. To emphasise that it was war damage John Emlyn carried one of the unexploded German bombs through the town to the police station. On another occasion he was evacuating civilians from France and placed a number of women and children in his own cabin. German planes bombed and strafed the vessel, killing all the women and children that were in his quarters.

That both the Herbert boys went to sea is no surprise, as their father John was a master mariner, and their mother was from the Enos maritime family. Both the brothers had certainly done their duty. One paid with his life.

Alan and Glyn Jones

Alan Jones, the local electrician, who served on the *Myrtis* and other vessels, had to give up seafaring as the dust from the coal cargoes badly affected his health. However, his brother Glyn, who had been apprenticed as a ship-builder, was at sea for years on the *Cape Howe* and *Stanholm*. Both the brothers were popular local characters. I wonder what Glyn would think if he were alive today about house prices at Borth. I remember walking down the village on a blustery afternoon around 1960, when I met Glyn. He was on his faithful old bike, with a basket of tools in the front, and the almost permanent sheet of hardboard tucked under one arm: he favoured this building material above all else, and was fondly known as the 'Hardboard King'. Thank God he was a sailor, as with the wind channelling down various alleys, he had to virtually tack his way along as the hardboard 'sail' threatened to blow him off course. He stopped, full of consternation, exclaiming loudly, 'I can't believe it!' He was so flabbergasted it took him a while to explain his state of excitement. The cottage Sabrina had just been sold for the unheard-of sum of £1,000 and Glyn was at pains to tell me that ten years previously he could have brought it for £200, but he did not think it was a bargain even then.

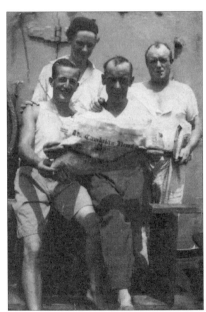

Left to right: Glyn Jones, John Davies, Jac Shami; back, Gwilym Davies

The Enos Family

The Enos family can be traced back to the 1600s, living in the Tresaith area, with an Owen Enos living at Esgair Eithin Farm. James Enos (1769–1860), was the first to become a master mariner. His eldest son John (1825–1908) lived in Borth at Berlin House, renamed Break House after World War One began, married Elizabeth Jones, and together they had five children. Another son Owen (b. 1828) was a mariner who died in 1895, and is buried in Barry. Another son Thomas (b. 1830) married Mary Morgan in 1855 and they had six children, two of whom died at sea: 24-year-old John in 1879 whilst serving on the *Snowdon*, and sixty-year-old David James, in 1920, whilst on the *Maindy Grange*. A daughter Jane (b. 1836) married master mariner John Davies.

John Enos (b. 1825) of Berlin House had a son James (1862–1949) who gained his master's certificate in 1889 and commanded many vessels including the barque *Eos*, and the steamers *Glanrheidol* and *Knight Almoner*. James' sister Mary Jane (b. 1855) married Captain William Francis of Raglan House, who commanded the *Glanrheidol, Glantivy* and the *Eleanor Thomas*. William and Mary's son, Idwal Owen Francis (1903–1962) also became a master mariner and worked for the Orient Line. However, he decided to swallow the anchor early, and became a successful dentist in Surrey. Idwal's sons Robert Owen Francis (b. 1945) and John Francis (b. 1952) both had careers at sea, Robert in the Royal Navy and John in the Merchant Navy. Another of James Enos' sisters, Margarita, married Captain John Herbert and produced two sons who became master mariners, John Emlyn and Lewis James.

There were another three brothers who were seafarers: Captain John Enos, Glanydon House, and Captain J. Owen Enos (1868–1938), master of the *Glanystwyth, Glanhavren, Cheltonian* and the *Knight of Saint John*. The *Cheltonian* was torpedoed in 1917, and J. Owen was held as prisoner of war in Germany. John received a letter at Glanydon informing him that his brother was a prisoner of the Germans at Karlsruhe, and that he was in good health, despite having been kept on the submarine that captured him for over eighteen days. Lewis James Herbert, his nephew, was on the same vessel and landed safely in France avoiding capture. Their other brother Lewis Enos (1860–1881) died at sea on the *Eos* at twenty-one years old and is buried at Malta.

Other Borth family members were the brothers James (1852-69), Thomas Charles Enos (1856–1946) and Owen Enos (1862–1943). Seventeen-year-old James drowned at sea on the barque *Cape Wrath*, Thomas became a master mariner and Owen moved to live at Barry. Thomas Charles (b. 1856) had a son who also became a master mariner with the same name as his father. Thomas Charles (1889–1952), always known as Charlie, had a distinguished career for which he was awarded an OBE and many service medals. He in turn had a son, Alan Charles Enos (b. 1932), who became a master mariner, and is the provider of much of this information. As Alan remarks, he is the fifth generation Enos originating from Borth, a fact of which he is immensely proud.

The previously-mentioned Thomas Charles Enos (b. 1856) had a full and adventurous life. As a child he devoted much of his time trying to get out of going to school, to the chagrin of his parents. However, coming from a family of mariners, it was no surprise that at the age of twelve he ran away to sea on a local schooner. For the next four years he learned the rudiments of seamanship the hard way. At sixteen years old he joined the *Sarah Ann* of Cardigan, a brigantine which voyaged to the West Indies. Thomas then went on a series of full rigged ships, the *Quebec* and *Mohur*, both of Windsor Nova Scotia, and then the Borth owned barque *Dora Ann*. He ended up on the west coast of South America in Peru, at a time when there was a war going on between Peru and Chile. Realising that the Peruvian Navy pay was more than his then current wage, his 'Cardi' spirit led him to join the Peruvian Navy. Throughout that conflict he served on the *Atualpa*. The countries brokered a peace and consequently Peruvian Navy life became boring.

Thomas then joined a United States schooner, and served in several vessels, amongst which was the *Vigilant*, trading between the USA and the West Indies. A stint ashore followed, no doubt fuelled by the attractive wages being offered in North America. For the next three years he was rigging derricks for the building of the New York Lake Erie Railway to Buffalo. Fifteen years had passed since he had sailed from Cardigan.

Steamships seemed to have been his next attraction, as he served for a time with the Atlas Line of New York, voyaging to the West Indies. The lure of his homeland was too much for him and he returned to Wales. His next ship was the *SS City of Truro*. He then went back to sail and joined the barquentine *Emblyn* of Ipswich, on a voyage to the River Plate, South America. His next vessels were the steamships *Restormal* and the *Godmunding* belonging to Cory & Sons.

By this time he was married. No doubt his wife Elizabeth was a settling influence on him, pushing his ambitions as he soon obtained his second mate's certificate. After a voyage on the *Lady Clive*, another Cory vessel, he was employed by Morel Ltd, and stayed with them for twenty-nine years. He voyaged on the *Ferncliffe Gardappi, Laboroure, Charles W. Anderson* and *Wenvoe*. By 1887 he gained his first command the *Beynon*, followed by the *Hart, Treherbert, Ninian Stuart, Portugalete, Lesreaulx* and the *Southerndown*. The latter vessel he commanded during the First World War, running from North America to France. His next employers were Llewelyn, Merrett & Price, and he commanded the *Glamorgan, Cliftonhall* and the *Maindy Grange*. That he managed to run all those ships and produce four boys and

Captain Thomas C 'Charlie' Enos (1889–1952)

93

six girls is a testament to his stamina if nothing else. He lived a crammed, eventful and adventurous life to ninety years old.

His son Thomas Charles, 'Charlie' (1889–1952), was highly decorated for services in both World Wars. He had a meteoric rise through the ranks that saw him as second mate in 1910, first mate in 1912 and extra master in 1915. At twenty-six years old he was one of the youngest ever extra masters from Wales. He began life at sea as a sixteen year old on the SS *Treherbert*, and for the next five years served on the steamers *Norisement*, *Harrovian* and *Cottonwood*. As an officer he was on the *Atlanton*, *Westergate*, *Cloughton*, *Empire Porpoise* and the *Putney Bridge* before gaining his extra master's certificate. From 1922-28 he was captain of the Oakfield and from 1937-45 he commanded the *Sheaf Holme*.

At the end of the war, and having garnered many awards and decorations, he thought he would retire as he was plagued with ulcers. The death of his son Brian in 1945, in a drowning accident at Langorse lake, Brecon, had already dealt him a heavy blow. However, in 1947 he was persuaded to join the Greek company Lyras & Lemos. Whilst commanding the *John Lyras* he supplied armaments for the Korean War. His maritime career ended when he was flown home from Kobe in Japan after becoming ill in 1952. Charlie had successfully avoided the enemy in two world wars and the conflict on the Korean Peninsula, which was as much down to luck as his skilled seamanship. What makes his story even more remarkable is the fact that he had spent ten years ashore in the 1930s trying to make a living from several business ventures, including a fish and chip shop. As his son Alan states, 'There are few shore jobs for a ship's captain', and he is convinced that it all caught up with his father, who died at the age of sixty-three in 1952.

On one memorable voyage Charlie had a very sick crew-member to deal with. After consulting the medical books he realised to his horror that the crewman had appendicitis. This meant an immediate operation in mid-ocean or death. Communications were only possible via Morse code, so Charlie decided to operate with the limited surgical knives in the first aid kit. After a hazardous couple of hours with the instructions being relayed to him via the radio officer, the primitive procedure was completed. Much to everyone's relief the patient made a full recovery with the captain, according to his son

Alan, praying to God it would never happen again.

In 1919 Charlie's ship was loading grain at a Black Sea port. The interpreter for the Russian Government agents, who liaised with the captain and was always accompanied by an armed guard, had been the mill-owner prior to the Communist government taking over. On the first day having finished discussing cargo details, the interpreter made an unusual request. He explained to the young captain that his wife and children had escaped from Russia and now lived in Belgium. As he probably would never see them again could the captain do him a great service? As the accompanying Russian guard did not understand English the interpreter went on to elaborate, stating that he would leave a small parcel the following day that contained a trove of family jewellery that the Russian authorities were unaware of. Charlie agreed to be entrusted with taking them to Europe, having them valued, selling them, and ensuring that the proceeds reached his family. Charlie kept his side of the bargain. The Welshman and the Russian only met once; Charlie often wondered what fate befell the parties concerned.

Another odd incident occurred in 1940 when Charlie was in Alexandria in command of the *Sheaf Holme*. He was ordered to voyage to Liverpool by the long route via the Cape of Good Hope, after accommodating an English 'ornithologist', Peter Cheesborough. The captain got on very well with the new passenger during the trip home and they exchanged addresses after arriving safely at Liverpool. In 1946 a letter arrived from Peter Cheeseborough explaining that he had actually been on a spying mission on the Turkish/Russian border, and not birdwatching in Egypt. This revelation was not as surprising as the strange sequel twenty years after Charlie's death. In 1972 Charlie's son Alan and his wife Valerie were visiting a friend at Magor, in south Wales. During this time Valerie got to know the next-door neighbour, a garage-owner, and in a conversation he stated that he was going on a trip to London to see his girlfriend who lived with her mother. Apparently the mother was courting a man called Peter Cheeseborough. Valerie related this fact to her husband as she was familiar with the spy story. Whilst both thought it was coincidental, they were still curious and asked if the garage-owner would ask this Peter Cheesborough a few questions and mention the name Captain Enos. Sure enough it was the spy Peter Cheeseborough, by then in his seventies and working as a janitor in a block of flats – he even sent a letter confirming his identity.

Captain T. C. Enos' son Alan (b. 1932) went to sea in 1950. Four years later he became second mate. Then, like a repeat of his father's career, he stayed ashore for nearly two decades employed as a representative of companies such as Avery Scales and Esso Petroleum, intermittently running a fruit shop and an antiques gallery. He returned to sea in 1973, soon became first mate, and gained his master's in 1978 whilst he was first officer on the *Viterwyck*. A year later he was in command of the *Playas*. He commanded the *Deseado, Brittany, Loch Fyne, Highland Princess, Potaro, Geest Star, Geest Bay, Geest Crest* and *Geest Cape*.

Again it seems that Borth was the catalyst for most of the sixteen mariners in this family, and it is the one vessel, the barque *Eos*, that seems to have been pivotal. The Enos seafarers of Borth constituted the nucleus of the crew of this Aberystwyth vessel, which was trading further afield than British waters and often voyaged to South America to places such as Rio Grande de Sul in Brazil.

The *Eos* was originally owned by Thomas H. Jones of Aberystwyth, and captained by his brother Samuel Jones. Four of the Enos boys, John, Lewis, James and Owen, were constant crew-members, with John as first mate. Finally in 1884, after gaining his master's certificate, John Enos bought and ran this ship. It became a training vessel for a generation of Enos masters who went on to command steamers. The *Eos* was wrecked, as were several other vessels, when navigation aids had moved, or been misplaced, in Safi Bay Morocco. Captain Jenkins of Borth, master of the *Eos* during this last voyage, was bought back to Britain on the *Tasmania* with his crew, and others from several wrecks. From humble yet enterprising beginnings in a small village, the Enos family became involved with shipping at Aberystwyth, Barry and Cardiff, where many of their descendants now continue the seafaring tradition.

The Jones Family (Surrey and Glendower); the Lewis Family (Dalston)

The German U-boat U91, under the command of Captain Von Glasenapp, went on a deadly voyage between 15 September and the end of October, 1918. It sailed from Heligoland to the Hebrides, then down the coasts of France and Spain, and returned to Germany through the Pentland Firth. During its murderous mission, it hunted down and sank twelve vessels, some of which were from neutral countries. Amongst them were the small French sailing vessels *Thérèse et Marthe, Ave Maris Stella, Maria Emmanuel, Maja* and the *Pierre*, as well as Spanish steamer *Mercedes*, the Portuguese steamer *Cazengo*, the Norwegian steamer *Luksefjell*, and tragically for three Borth families the 1,963 ton *SS Heathpark*, which was carrying iron ore from Bilbao to Maryport in Cumbria.

This recently built vessel, owned by the Denholm Brothers, of Greenock, was torpedoed at 3 am on 5 October 1918, just off the coast near Bilbao, with the loss of all twenty-five crew-members including Borth men Captain Hugh Jones, Seaview; David Llewelyn Lewis, bosun, of Dalston House; David Kenneth Jones deck boy, Glanmor House, who was the captain's nephew, and another nephew William Roberts, who had recently moved to live at Liverpool. Only the body of Captain Jones was recovered

Captain Hugh Jones (1874–1918), commander of many Park vessels

by the fishing vessel *Isabelita*, of Ondarroa. He was buried in that little Basque fishing village, but in 1925 his body was re-buried at Bilbao by the Commonwealth Graves Commission.

Captain Hugh Jones (1874–1918), commander of the *SS Surrey, Cathcartpark, Garvelpark, Wellpark, Mountpark, Holmpark* and the *Heathpark*, was one of five brothers who came from an illustrious seafaring family. Two of his brothers also became master mariners: Edward (1864–1925), who commanded the *Mountpark, Beechpark* and other *Park* vessels until 1923, and Morgan Hugh (1875–1925), who was captain of the *Cadeby*, and the *SS Ashton*. Morgan was in command of the 1,330 ton *Cadeby* carrying a cargo of pitwood from Oporto to Cardiff when she was stopped by a German submarine, and the crew ordered to take to the boats. Immediately thereafter the vessel was sunk. There were four passengers and sixteen crew-members in the boats; as well as the captain, there were Borth crewmen John D. Thomas of Eversleigh House and David Jenkins of Rock House. They were rescued by the crew of the *Bonafide* of Penzance, and were landed at Newlyn, Cornwall.

The other brothers were David Hugh (1863–1935) who was first mate on the *SS Beechpark* when it was torpedoed in 1917, and John (1868–1884), who was washed overboard and drowned at sixteen years old on his first voyage. Their father was David Jones (1837–1891), master mariner, who had married Ann Hughes in 1861, and built the family home Seaview, today's Maesafor, in the same year as his marriage.

By 1895, Captain Hugh Jones' wife Annie owned land on which the houses Surrey, Glendower, Glanmor and Carron were built. Captain Edward Jones lived at Glanmor, Captain Morgan H. Jones at Glendower, Captain Hugh Jones at Surrey, which was named after his first command *SS Surrey*, and first officer David H. Jones lived at No.8 Cambrian Terrace whilst in Borth, and at South Pacific, at Barry Dock, South Wales. David Hugh served as first mate on the *SS Maggie Hough, SS Samuel Hough* and the *SS Glenmoor* of Newcastle. One of his sons, David Idwal, was at sea for a short time.

Strange to relate, two of the Borth victims of the *Heathpark* had already survived a torpedo attack. David Kenneth Jones had been with his father Captain Edward Jones on the *SS Beechpark* when she was struck in August 1917; though she sank rapidly all the crew was saved. *SS Heathpark* crew-member David Llewelyn Lewis (b. 1892) had also survived a sinking at the beginning of the final year of the war. On a Friday night in March 1918 the German U-boat 105 torpedoed the *SS Penvean*, 15 miles north west of South Stack Rock, Holyhead. Twenty-two of the crew were killed. Three were from Borth: Hugh James Manchester House, son of Captain H. James Scranton; Morgan Morgan, Gogerddan Gardens Ynyslas, and Basil Lougher Davies, son of Captain T. Davies Gloucester House. Another Borth man, David Llewellyn Lewis of Dalston House, was landed in an exhausted condition, and was hospitalized in north Wales for a few days until he was able to proceed home to Borth. Seven months later, in October 1918, he was torpedoed again, and this time did not survive.

Amongst the tragedies, there were also a number of narrow escapes. It is noticeable in the terse reports in the *Cambrian News* that quite a few Borth men survived not one, but several sinkings bought about by enemy action. They seemed to have taken it all in their stride, and it must have taken a certain resilience for them to return to sea, sometimes within weeks of a sinking.

David Llewelyn Lewis' two brothers Evan and Alfred were also seafarers. Alfred served under many Borth men including Captains Herbert, Edwards and Enos. He had first gone to sea with Captain Lewis Williams Picton House, with Borth shipmates T. Tibbot, D. Jones, J. Davies, I. Williams and D. Jenkins. During the 1930s Alfred was a regular crew-member on the *SS Goodig*, a vessel owned by Stone & Rolf. Evan William Lewis (1892–1940) survived the First World War at sea, where at, one time, he was in the RNVR. Tragically in 1940, he lost his life on the *SS Bradfyne* along with a relative Raymond Hughes (1924–1940). Of the three Lewis brothers, only Alfred survived these major conflicts.

Women of Borth

As research testifies, village women were courageous, hardy and stoic. They had to be, as their lives were constantly being held to ransom by the vagaries of seafaring, which left many of them widows. Infant mortality was a constant spectre, whether it was due to diseases of the time, or children, some as young as eight, drowning whilst working at sea. One Borth mother was prevented from seeing her ten-year-old son's body, badly disfigured after submersion for several days following the wrecking of the sloop *Venus* in the Dyfi entrance on a stormy morning in November 1857.

Captain James lost his fourteen-year-old son Enoch when he fell overboard from the *Dovey Belle* and drowned as the vessel was lying off Gravesend. Young David Morgan, son of Captain John Morgan, died at sea in 1880 on the schooner *Meirion Lass*, a vessel that his proud father had bought for them. Jane Jones lost both husband and son whilst they were on a voyage together in 1891. It is sobering to think that up to 1940 there were more than twice as many fatalities at sea than there were in coal mining. Added to all this uncertainty was the women's daily chore of providing sustenance for often large families. Life was precarious: the mainstay until the twentieth century, the herring, was seasonal, and its harvesting was hazardous. Often women arranged with nearby farmers to grow a row or two of potatoes in exchange for labour or herrings. Vestiges of such activities are still visible in a Bryn Bwl Farm field.

In the early days, the villagers had to adapt themselves to these conditions. There was a whole group of shrimping and cockling ladies, who supplemented their diet by trading their catch for loaves of bread at the market in Aberystwyth. One such woman was Ann Hughes, who lived in an earth-and-thatch cottage opposite today's Evelwen. This site was surrounded by a midden of cockleshells. Ann's cottage was destroyed during a fierce storm at the end of the nineteenth century. Mary Hughes lost husband John and two sons when they drowned in 1845 whilst on the *Betsy*, leaving her with five children to raise at the Friendship Inn.

Eleanor Hughes was a widow with three children. She lost her husband Thomas when he drowned whilst commanding the *Eleanor* on a voyage from Caernarvon to Aberdyfi in 1820. From then on Eleanor eked out a living carrying turf seven miles to Aberystwyth each day to sell at the markets. All this hard labour eventually took its toll. In her mid 60s she made a petition to Trinity House for financial assistance. In this she was championed by Captains Enoch James of the *Mary & Ellen*, Richard Davies of the *Hope*, Hugh Davies of the *Elizabeth* and John Hughes of the *Virtue*, demonstrating the supportive nature of the maritime community at Borth.

Whenever they could, the womenfolk joined their husbands on coastal sloops as crew-members. Brothers John and Hugh Davies often took their wives and daughters on the family owned vessels *Sarah, France* and the *Amity*, in the 1830s. John Evans captain of the sloop *Mermaid*, undoubtedly took his wife, as she gave birth on board to the appropriately-named John Seaborn Evans in 1822.

Captain Abraham Davies took his wife Mary on the 240-ton brig *Ethel Ann*. Captain David Jones of the schooner *Resolute*, with his nineteen-year-old son as mate, often took his daughter Mary Jane on voyages with them. Captain Edward Edwards (b. 1823) took his wife Anne and his daughter Sarah Sophia on the barques *Eurydice* and the *Walton*. Captain John Davies (b. 1834) was accompanied by his wife Catherine on the schooner *Ocean Wave*, and possibly on other vessels he commanded, such as *Miss Evans* and the *Sydney & Jane*. Captain Richard Jenkins took his whole family with him on the 80-ton schooner *Ceylon* in 1861; they were his thirty-one year old wife Mary, daughter Mary aged eleven, and son Richard aged eight. In the 1870s Captain Richard Davies took his wife Jane, and six-month-old daughter Elizabeth on the *Rachel Lewis*.

Captain John Williams was accompanied by his wife Anne on many voyages on the barques *Granville* and *General Picton*, to India, Australia and New Zealand. The captain had a business partner and friend with the surname of Mackenzie in New Zealand, and some of his children bore the name Mackenzie. Anne came back from her first voyage and gave birth to her eldest son John, and after a second voyage to India, she came back and had a daughter Anne Granville. Anne jokingly claimed that her daughter's dark complexion was because she had been conceived in the tropics. The *General Picton* was lost in mid Pacific as her cargo of coal ignited, and she had to be abandoned. Although there was no loss of life, the captain was deeply affected by the loss of this vessel in 1888; four years later he died. His brother Captain David Williams (1849–1910), took his daughter Elsie on voyages to the Baltic and the Mediterranean on the *Glenholm* and *Earl Cadogan*. Elsie would join her father when his ship berthed at Liverpool.

In the 1880s Captain William Richards took his wife and occasionally his daughters on the SS *Lady Mostyn* and SS *Eira*. His daughter Elizabeth went on one voyage from Newport to London as a stewardess, as her discharge papers prove. Later she became a major figure in the suffragette movement. Both vessels had monogrammed crockery, and a plate from the *Eira* still exists.

Thomas Charles Enos (1856–1946) had lived a very adventurous life before he met and married his wife. He had voyaged the world's oceans in sail and steam as well as working ashore, building railways in America. For a few years he had even served in the Peruvian navy. This intelligent, yet hitherto unambitious devil-may-care mariner was to change tack after meeting the beautiful Elizabeth Davidson. She was the daughter of a Cwmystwyth lead miner whose family originated from Alston in Cumbria. The redoubtable Elizabeth insisted that Thomas better himself before she would marry him. Thomas readily agreed and rapidly worked his way up the ranks to become a master mariner. Elizabeth accompanied him on many voyages and their union produced ten children, one of whom, named like his father

Elizabeth Davidson from Cwmystwyth bore ten children to Captain Thomas Charles Enos (1856–1946)

Thomas Charles and known as Charlie, also became a master mariner.

No doubt the womenfolk had an input in providing some vestiges of home comforts on the larger vessels. Captain Alan Enos recalls that his mother, during a long voyage to South America, had passed away the time making a set of lace antimacassars which she proudly had on the settee and chairs. As the ship was approaching Britain her husband Captain 'Charlie' Enos, told his wife to put away these covers lest the owners thought that he and his wife were masquerading as owners themselves.

Thomas Charles 'Charlie' Enos (1889–1952) took his wife Violet with him to Buenos Aires on their honeymoon. The sea was in her blood as she was from an old Newquay Ceredigion maritime family. They went together on several other voyages to Russia, the Mediterranean and Canada. However, such voyages were limited as Thomas sailed for over fifteen years during hostilities in both world wars and the Korean conflict. The Enos women often accompanied their husbands to sea, and this tradition continued with the fifth generation and the last master mariner Captain Alan Enos.

Alan Enos took his wife Valerie with him as often as possible, and she became adept at living on board and familiar with maritime terminology. Valerie would join Alan at places such as Hamburg, Panama, Miami, New York and New Orleans, and voyaged to South Africa, South America, Russia, the Middle East and the USA. She was usually signed on as either nurse or chief steward. Occasionally Valerie had to organise receptions for visitors to the ship. As she explained, she was essentially doing a PR exercise for the shipping company. Valerie recalls that on one occasion when she arrived to join Alan's ship it was tied alongside several others. Having arrived at quayside all dressed up, with accompanying luggage, she had to climb up and down and across other vessels to access Alan's ship: quite a feat in high heels. Valerie arrived somewhat dishevelled, ladders in her stockings and streaming with sweat … not her intended glamorous arrival. Other than being a company hostess and chief steward, she frequently kept watch and obviously thoroughly enjoyed these adventures.

Captain Thomas Davies took his daughter on many trips on his schooners *Nathaniel* and *Pluvier* and on one occasion had a 'passenger', his wife Mary J. Davies, with him on the *Nathaniel*, on a coastal voyage. Captain John Davies, Bodina House, took his wife Mary Jane on voyages on the *King David* and the *King Cadwallon* before the First World War. Captain Horace I. Jones was accompanied by his wife on the *SS Cape Sable* in the 1930s. Captain Roberts often took his wife Mary, on the *Oronsay* in the 1950s. I remember meeting bosun Harry Jones of Panteg, and his wife Anne, on board the *Asian Renown* in Australia in the early 1970s.

Rosaline, wife of ship's engineer Marcus Evans, often accompanied him on Caltex tankers in the 1970s and 1980s, visiting Sumatra, India, Bahrain and the Caribbean. One of the voyages lasted fifteen months. When one of the tankers was in dry dock for three months in Japan, Rosaline took the opportunity to explore the country and go on the famous bullet train. Her status was 'supernumerary': she was apparently supposed to receive one shilling per voyage. Rosaline was usually the only woman on board, so she was glad to meet up with another officers' wives when docked in port. On one occasion she remembers meeting two women who were travelling with their husbands on the same ship. It appeared that these two ladies did not hit it off, and Rosaline was relieved not to be in the same situation.

A relative of Marcus', John Whitlock Davies, another ship's engineer, took his wife Myra with him on two Elder Dempster ships, the *MV Fourah Bay* and *MV Fulani*. The crew, including wives of senior officers, would fly from Liverpool to Rotterdam, and sail from there to Amsterdam, Antwerp, Bremmen and Hamburg, discharging and loading cargo, for West Africa. Some of the wives would leave the ship at the last European loading port, whilst others would go on the full trip.

What, one may ask, did Captain John Evans' wife Jane, think of events in 1882 – in fact was she complicit in them? Captain Evans (1828–94) took his wife with him on the *Rowland Evans*, a 209-ton brig, in which he was a major shareholder with a mortgage of £600 in her. This vessel was insured for £1,800. After leaving Antwerp with a cargo of silver sand, the captain claimed he had noticed that the ship was leaking whilst in dock and shortly after sailing. Apparently she then began to leak from an area which could not be reached internally. They got as far as Cardigan Bay, thirty miles opposite

Borth, when the captain stopped the vessel and ordered everyone, including his wife, to take to the ship's boat. Circling the *Rowland Evans* for a few hours, it was decided that she could be a threat to navigation; so two holes were drilled into the woodwork to scuttle her. A few hours later the boat reached Borth.

In the subsequent enquiry, the evidence of the mate corroborated that of the captain. However, the three crew-members contradicted this and stated that 'the pumps were dealing with the excess water, and that they knew nothing about the vessel having sprung a leak back in Antwerp'. They also stated: 'as they were familiar with Cardiganshire ports, the vessel could have easily accessed them'. One of the men put it succinctly when he said 'they disembarked from the boat right at the captain's front door'. The Court of Enquiry remarked that it was the clearest example of premature abandonment that the court had ever had come to its notice. Suffice to say, the captain's certificate was suspended for twelve months, and the mate was also censured. With no insurance payout, perhaps John Evans' intended retirement had to be postponed. He had been mate and captain of the *Sarah* over a period of five years until her loss in 1864. He then commanded the schooner *Eleanor & Jane* and in 1894 he drowned whilst commanding the barque *Nelson Hewertson*. His father was either Captain John Evans (b. 1797) who commanded the *Aberystwyth* in 1852, or another Captain John Evans (b. 1798), who ran the schooners *Angharad*, *Rose* and the *Hannah & Jane* in the 1860s. Another relative William Evans (b. 1858) was on the sailing vessel *Brazilian* as mate when he gained his master's certificate. He went on to command the steamers *Jerseymoor*, *Castlemoor*, *Raithmoor*, *Elmmoor*, *Sydney Reid*, *Western Valleys*, and *Frederick Cleaves* and continued at sea until he was well over seventy years old.

Many of the families in the nineteenth century were matriarchal because of the long absences of the men. Often, if widowed, the women had financial responsibility in part or sole ownership of a vessel. Therefore the women were often the business brain as well as the emotional heart of a family. As early as the 1770s, Jane Hugh owned half of the sloop *Providence* with Thomas Pryce owning the other. In 1786 she bequeathed her share to John Rees, the regular skipper. After the death of Captain Evan Jenkins, the sloop *Priscilla*, built at Ynyslas in 1845, belonged to his widow Anne, who ran it for a number of years before it was lost with all hands off Aberdaron in 1873. In 1871 Ann Jenkins became sole owner of the barque *Dorothy* after her husband, Captain Lewis Jenkins, died. She appointed her 32-year-old nephew, Captain John Jones, to run the vessel for her as he was an accomplished mariner who had previously commanded the schooner *Glad Tidings* and the barque *Alice*. Enoch James (1787–1856) bequeathed the sloop *Mary & Ellen* to his wife Mary (1789–1866). In the ten years after Captain James' death, she ran the sloop and eventually sold it. At the same time she managed to acquire the schooner *Resolute*, which she in turn left to her grandson.

Another of the James family, Captain David Enoch (1811–1870), left 4 shares each in the schooner *Eleanor* to his two elder sons, 2 shares each to his younger sons and 1 share each to his two daughters. Captain John James (1818–1884) gave the schooner *Dovey Belle* to his son John, subject to him paying his aunt Margaret £15 per year, with the proviso that on John's demise the vessel was to be given in equal parts to the grandchildren. The barque *Drusus*, owned by Captain David Rees, passed to his wife Elizabeth after his death in 1881. Elizabeth mortgaged the ship for £280, Margaret Thomas and Ann Davies being mortgagees with her. This arrangement lasted until the end of 1883 when the vessel was sold.

Captain David Daniel the younger (1793–1844) put his shares in the 65-ton schooner *Aquila* into a trust for his young daughters Elizabeth and Catherine. Ann Daniel (neé James), a widow, had 8 shares in the family schooner *Rosina*. Rosina Evans (neé Daniel) had shares in the *Martha Lloyd*, as did her master mariner brother James Watkin Daniel. He eventually sold his shares to Lewis Williams, a miner of Borth who produced four master mariner sons. Ships were bought and sold as well as the shares in them, involving many of the families and individuals in the wider Borth community.

One captain's wife had a remarkable life. Maggie Brown (1851–1940) was born in south Wales and went to America with her aunt at the age of six. When she was eighteen she married a John Williams of Scranton. Before a year had passed, her husband had died leaving her with a young child, John Watkin Williams. They moved from Scranton to San Francisco, and there Maggie met her second husband-to-be, Borth man Hugh James (1843–1916).

He had begun seafaring on local schooners, in particular the Borth-owned *Gleanor*, which was commanded by his father Captain David James. Hugh was captain of the barque *Hawarden Castle* at the time he met Maggie. They married in 1877, and they, and her son, returned from San Francisco on this vessel to live at 2 Picton Terrace, then later to a large new house, Scranton Villa (no doubt named by Maggie). The stepson, influenced by Captain James and Borth's seafaring ethos, became a master mariner and commanded Booth Line Vessels. He was honoured by the Liverpool & London War Risks Association Ltd. after successfully evading a submarine attack whilst in command of the *SS Benedict* in July 1918, where his seamanlike skills and courage were much appreciated, and he received a 100-guinea reward.

Hugh and Maggie seemed inseparable; they sailed together to all parts of the world for a number of years. On one voyage, which included rounding Cape Horn on the *Carmarthen Castle*, she gave birth to a son Hugh, five days out from Rangoon. They had eight children, two girls and six boys. Sadly two of the boys died within a year of birth: David at eight months and Richard Harold at twelve months. Later, another two sons died, Reginald, of tuberculosis at twenty-one years old, and then Hugh, who had been born at sea, also lost his life at sea in 1918 when his ship, the *Penvean*, was torpedoed. One of the daughters, Annie Bertha, married ship's engineer David Hugh Rees. This intrepid woman, who lived to be ninety, travelled the world and experienced many triumphs and tragedies.

Margaret Jones nee Williams (b. 1838), who married Captain David Jones of the *Ceres*, was herself part of a long line of mariners. Her father, husband, four brothers, two sons and uncles, were all seafarers, three of whom died away from home. Every time family members went off to sea she and other women in her situation would wonder, from bitter experience, if they would ever see their loved ones again. Her photograph reveals her to be self-composed and optimistic, yet the eyes betray a sense of sadness.

There must have been hundreds of women – mothers, wives, sweethearts or daughters – separated from their menfolk for long periods of time. Every stormy night at Borth must have been brought home to them how many dangerous miles of sea were between them and their loved ones. Spare a thought for the grief of Richard and

Mary Hughes who lost their sixteen-year-old mariner son William Thomas Hughes, in 1859. Captain David Hughes and his wife Elizabeth lost two sons, James at twenty-four years old and Evan at twenty-five: both drowned at sea. I remember dear old Mrs. Roberts who lived alone at Convoy House, which was full of wonderful souvenirs from the far corners of the globe. At the time I did not realise that she had lost both her husband, Captain Roberts, and their son, to the sea.

Also lost at sea was Richard Jenkins, son of Thomas (1805–93) and Rebecca (1807–76) of Pengoitan. Who now remembers, or knows, who seaman John Jones was? In 1883, he fell from the masthead of the *Dora Ann*, which was under the command of Captain Lloyd. His remains are lying somewhere between New Zealand and Chile in the vastness of the Pacific Ocean. Others are buried in Korea, India, China, Brazil, Argentina, Algeria, Spain, America and France. In 1883 young Morgan Lloyd, bosun on the *Nant Francon*, drowned nearer home in Swansea Dock, leaving a widow and child at Borth.

Conversely, in 1900, Captain Lewis returned from a voyage to Buenos Aires, whilst in command of the *SS Ashlands*, to find that his wife Kate had been buried.

The wife of Captain Richard Rees (1870–1918) of Morawel House had seen her husband only twice during the First World War. Towards the end of 1918 she must have thought that all would be well. Fate, however, struck a savage blow as she received a telegram to go to Glasgow where Richard had been suddenly taken ill on the *War Tabard*. By the time she arrived, he had died of pneumonia. He was the son of Captain Thomas Rees, Angorfa.

Nearer our time, one's heart goes out to the likes of seaman William Thomas' mother, who held the vain hope until her dying day, that he would return home to Borth. As previously stated, William had been lost in February 1941 in the aftermath of an attack on the *Clunepark* while his brother John could hear him calling for help but could do nothing. Mrs. Thomas believed that he had swum or drifted to a nearby island and suffered some sort of amnesia from which he would eventually recover and arrive back home.

Muriel Kind

Muriel Ernestine Thirza Kind, born in 1910, after private schooling, and against parental wishes, enrolled as a student nurse in Walton Hospital Liverpool. In 1939, with the outbreak of World War Two, she was appointed to the Royal Naval Hospital at Devonport, Plymouth. A month later she was part of a medical team rushed to Scapa Flow in the Orkneys, following the sinking of *HMS Royal Oak*. At Scapa Flow she served aboard the hospital ships *Alba*, an ex Elder Dempster line, and the *Isle of Jersey*, previously a Southern Rail cross-channel ferry. These vessels patrolled the North Sea and transported convoy survivors to the naval hospital at Aberdeen. For this work she was one of the few women to be awarded the Atlantic Star.

Muriel was next appointed to the Royal Naval Hospital at Barrow Gurney, near Bristol, for a year, then to HMS Blackcap, a Fleet Air Arm base at Stretton in Lancashire. She received a further three medals for her wartime services.

Muriel lived at The Anchorage, and it was here that she developed a strong rapport with her relative and godson David Tink. Their many happy hours talking about ships and sailors no doubt influenced young David, as he was to have an illustrious career at sea and in the Fleet Air Arm. Muriel was a lifelong supporter of the RNLI at Borth, and she received the RNLI Silver Medal for thirty years' service. It would seem inevitable that, in accordance with her wishes, her ashes were scattered in Borth Bay in 2006, by the crew of the inshore rescue boat.

Dorothy Toler

Dorothy Toler (b. 1916) was the youngest of three children. Her father was a Second Lieutenant in the RASC but she never knew her parents. As they were returning to Liverpool in 1918 on the *RMS Leinster*, the vessel was torpedoed and sunk off Dublin Bay. The children were 'farmed out' to family, the elder two staying together while Dorothy went to a childless couple. Later she trained as a nurse at Great Ormond Street Hospital.

At the start of World War Two, Dorothy joined the WRNS and became a member of Coastal Forces with the rank of petty officer, based at Hornet, Boscawen and Kestral as a driver. After a few driving lessons she was questioned on her driving skills and mechanical knowledge, and must obviously have given a good account of herself. Consequently, she was allocated a three-ton Bedford lorry to deliver new MTB/MGB engines and collect damaged engines for repair. In later years, she would claim not to know a spanner from a tyre lever!

After the war, a chance conversation with her next-door neighbour Miss Hyatt led to a summer job at a café in Dolybont. It was there that she met her husband Robert Toler, who had a long association with Borth which had begun with camping holidays at Ynyslas as a young man, and later working in the lead mines.

Dorothy was a keen supporter of the Lifeboat and became involved with the Borth Ladies Guild when it was formed, serving on the committee. In later years, she helped in the Lifeboat shop, therefore maintaining the nautical link. She also served as vicar's warden in St. Mathew's church, and was a member of the Cardiganshire Horticultural Society.

Yvette Ellis-Clark

Yvette Ellis-Clark (b. 1962) lived with her parents in Rock Villa on the cliff. Even though the sea was an ever-present element throughout her childhood, it was not until several of her friends joined the Navy that she seriously considered a maritime career. This would also dovetail with her passion for travelling. Just before she was eighteen she applied to join the Women's Royal Navy Service, and opted to become a Weapons Analyst, which seemed appropriate as she loved mathematics (a requirement for the job).

Nothing happened for nearly three years, and then one morning, on St David's Day, she woke up to a telephone call from an official from the Royal Navy asking if she was still interested in joining the service. Despite the surprise of it, she immediately said yes. She was told to report to Plymouth on 23 May 1983 – a day that coincided with her family going to a wedding at Bristol. Yvette attended the wedding then bid everyone farewell and reported for training at HMS Raleigh, where she joined Group Class Victory 21.

This was the start of a twenty-three year naval career. Specialist training in communications took place at HMS Dryad and Fraser Gunnery Range. Yvette spent the next eighteen months in London, at Whitehall. During this time she enjoyed a two-month secondment to Norway working with the Royal Marines, some of whom were from Talybont and Aberystwyth. Working shifts of twenty-four hours on and twenty-four hours off gave her plenty of time to get her first taste of ski-ing, learning both downhill and cross-country. On her return, she had another secondment, giving her a chance to work with the RAF at Rudloe Manor. Then she moved to Northwood to work with highly sensitive communications, and it was here that she met up with Peter Norrington-Davies of Dolybont. During her career, Yvette was to meet up with others from the Borth area, including Robert Patterson-Jones, Simon Moss, Paul Thomas, Eryl Morris, Tony Evans, Harry Hughes and Tony Hosell.

For her next eighteen-month draft she was sent to Gibraltar.

Here she advanced to Leading Wren. Yvette then returned to Whitehall, stopping briefly at HMS Royal Arthur to complete a leadership course, which she found quite gruelling. She then took the Leading Wrens' Communications course at HMS Mercury, which she sailed through, winning the Herbert Lott award for best student of the year.

One day in March 1990, whilst home on leave, Yvette was having breakfast and her father Ebbie was reading the *Western Mail*, when he said 'Girls are going to sea, then.'

'No way,' said Yvette, as she had heard nothing of this previously. On her return to Whitehall she found out it was true and they were asking for female volunteers to go to sea. Yvette jumped at the chance and joined the first contingent of Wrens to go through Specialist Sea Training. This included firefighting and damage control, all of which was very new to Yvette. She then had to do a nine-week conversion course to combine her shore communications knowledge with that of shipgoing equipment and communications .

She was very pleased to learn that she was to join *HMS Brilliant*, the first ship to take female crew-members. Her position by then was Leading Radio Operator. The programme included a trip to the Gulf, and Yvette was the first Borth Wren to go to sea and into a war zone. The mindless devastation made an indelible mark on her. Everything seemed wrecked, with immense oil fires still burning, as well as body parts floating near areas where mines had been laid. The horror was bought home when a boatload of matelots went on patrol and a few of the younger ones returned traumatised by the sights they saw.

Yvette enjoyed the seagoing experience immensely. The fact that men and women shared facilities in close proximity was an issue sensationalised out of all proportion by the press. As she states, 'It does not matter what the women did, it was headlines'. A case in point was when *HMS Brilliant* went to the aid of a merchant ship which had developed an engine room fire. It took three days for the vessel to be safely towed back to port after extinguishing the fire. Despite the fact that the majority of the crew were males, and were the main participants in this event, the press report stated, 'Seventeen Wrens fight fire'.

During her career, Yvette was awarded four medals, the Gulf

Medal with a rose inset, NATO Medal, Queens Golden Jubilee Medal and a Good Conduct Medal. She received the NATO Medal after doing a three-month stint on the *HMS Invincible* in Bosnia. She recalls spending so much time at the bar that she was awarded a hip flask, usually given only after two years of patronage. The *Invincible*, an aircraft carrier, was too big for her liking, with too many crew-members making it impossible to have a sense of true camaraderie. The one redeeming feature was that they baked their own bread every day for afternoon tea, known as 'four o'clockers'.

It was around this time that she met her husband-to-be, Tim Clark, at a forces rugby match. He was a marine engineering mechanic serving on *HMS Herald*. Theirs was, initially, a distant and mainly secret courtship; only cards were exchanged, and they managed just once to go out to dinner.

After returning on the *HMS Endurance* from one of her Antarctic voyages, Tim and Yvette got married in Borth church. Her hen-night was held on board ship, and was quite unique as all the 'hens' were her male colleagues dressed as women. Yvette left the *Endurance* before Tim, and was based at a NATO shore-base in Portugal at Oeiras, just outside Lisbon. For the next four years, they saw each other at holiday times and weekends. While in Portugal, Yvette's near neighbour was Borth man Oliver Evans and his wife Barbara. Oliver is the brother of Gethin and Jac Evans, both profiled later.

Yvette became Permanent Staff Instructor at the shore based HMS Cambria. Her duties encompassed organising Royal Naval

Tim and Yvette Ellis-Clark,
married at last after their largely secret courtship

Reserve units that were away on courses. Tim was now on *HMS Richmond*, which was on deployment to the Mediterranean and the Caribbean. By now, Tim and Yvette had a son Dion, and it was decided that Tim would leave the Navy and become a househusband. Yvette continued in the service, and was based at Northwood in London at the Permanent Joint Headquarters of the Services. After twenty-three years service Tim, Yvette and Dion returned to live at the family home, Rock Villa. During her many travels she met several people with Borth connections, amongst them Eirwen, sister of Ella Jenkins of Gwastad, and Elizabeth Rodaway-Baker in Guernsey. Yvette has kept up her interest in the sea by working for the RNLI as a box secretary, and always loves the opportunity to get together with old shipmates.

The Lloyd Family (Frondirion)

There have been innumerable mariners from the Lloyd family, going back to at least the early 1700s. They feature constantly in Borth's seagoing history. They, like many other extended Borth families, moved from house to house as well as constructing new houses as fortunes and family sizes waxed and waned. The Lloyds were to be found at certain times over the last two centuries at Cwmcethin, Glanwern House, Lerry House, Mayfield, Resolute, Inman Cottage, Y Graig and Frondirion.

Derek Lloyd (b. 1918) was on the *SS Sarastone* in the 1930s, which was occasionally captained by Eli Robilliard, who lived at Torteval Borth, with Derek's father, Edward Lewis Lloyd as second officer. This vessel ran Franco's blockade during the Spanish Civil War to take food and supplies in to Spain and bring refugees out. Before going to sea, Derek bought a camera from Boots the Chemist, Aberystwyth and took many photographs of this vessel and the various crews who came from Swansea, Llanelli, Aberaeron, Aberarth, Llanon and, of course, Borth. It is quite touching that he can affectionately recall all their names, including those of the Indian stokers.

The *Sarastone* was a 5,000-ton coaster with foreign-going articles owned by Stone and Rolf of Swansea. This vessel would 'tramp' anywhere, and Derek remembers delivering a cargo of anthracite to Iceland for that country's fishing fleet, and delivering coal to Northern Russia as well as voyaging to Mediterranean ports as far as Yugoslavia.

Derek left the sea in 1938 and was involved in the founding of the Borth power station, which bought electricity to the village. He spent World War Two in a munitions factory in the Midlands and returned, after hostilities ceased, to Borth where he was a postman up until his retirement.

Derek's two brothers, John (b. 1922) and Edward (b. 1920)

began their careers as cadets with J. C. Harrison, a London company. Edward went to sea in 1937, and on his third voyage in 1940 he witnessed the battle of the River Plate, and the blowing up of the *Graf Spee*, from the bridge of the *Harperley*. He served on nine of this company's vessels and left in 1952 as first mate.

Edward then joined Common Brothers of Newcastle upon Tyne, and served out his career with them on some of the largest ore carriers and tanker vessels afloat at the time. In 1954 he gained his master's ticket and his first command was the *Kurdistan*. The largest vessel he captained was the 225,000-ton tanker *Fina Britannia* in 1971, which was one of the biggest tankers in the world at that time. He had previously been in charge of the 208,900-ton *Al Badih* and the 208,800-ton *Arabiyah*. He, like his father, spent most of his life at sea. As Captain L. J. Herbert mentions in his memoirs, circa 1970, 'I can only name one who is still sailing as master/captain ... Edward Lloyd, Frondirion Borth.' In 1978, he returned to the Fina Britannia as Commodore of the Fleet. He also captained *Border Regiment, Border Hunter, Warbah, Leeds, Newburn* and the *Strait of Canso*; the latter was his last command prior to retirement. Having his own pennant as commodore, Captain Edward Lloyd flies it proudly outside his home in Middlesborough.

Younger brother John did not like the poor pay as a cadet and decided to get some seagoing experience. He signed on as a deckhand on the *Harcalo*. John was soon a bosun and served on twenty vessels altogether, including the *Harmattan, Arowa, Eros, Empire Lord, Sunderland* and the *Vera Radcliffe*, about which John remarked, 'There was nothing to eat and plenty to do.' In the time-honoured Borth tradition, John named a bungalow that he built in his retirement, Durango, after his last ship. It was next to Rigi, in Francis Road, but recently his widow has moved to another location and taken the name with her. This is another Borth tradition, which often confuses researchers. After swallowing the anchor, John ended up running a milk retail business.

Another Lloyd brother, Lewis (b. 1916) was at sea for a time and also served on the *Sarastone*, but with the outbreak of the Second World War joined the RAF. I remember him well as the finest prawn-net maker in Borth. He was injured whilst serving the RAF during the war and was invalided out of service.

It is no wonder that all four brothers went to sea, as their father, Edward Lewis Lloyd (b. 1869), son of Lewis and Sarah Lloyd, of Leri House, Borth, had been a seaman all his working life. Like many others, he began his career just before the turn of the twentieth century on small sailing vessels in Cardigan Bay. At twelve years old he was on the 100-ton schooner *Nathaniel* with Captain John Davies (b. 1832) in command. He then moved swiftly on to the last of the great sailing ships voyaging from Glasgow Liverpool and Swansea to the west coast of South America, rounding Cape Horn several times before he was twenty-five years old.

As the age of steam was tolling the knell of the wind-driven ships, he joined the Canadian Northern Steamship Company, and by the age of twenty-eight became second officer. From 1916 to 1919, he was involved with the Cunard Steamship Company. Edward L. Lloyd was a classic example of a man who made light of the transition between sail and steam. As well as British ships, he also served on Dutch vessels, as at one time he was based in Rotterdam where he met his wife Arina.

He was to be involved in one of the maritime dramas of the age when in 1913, whilst serving on the German steamer the *SS Volturno*, owned by the Uranium Company Rotterdam, he became an instant hero by arguably preventing a major maritime tragedy. The *Volturno* was carrying 800 Russian and Polish

Edward L Lloyd (1869–1946), who 'made light of the transition between sail and steam'

emigrants to Halifax Nova Scotia. In mid-Atlantic the vessel encountered a severe gale, and to compound things, an explosion occurred, resulting in a fierce fire. The foremast was severely damaged, which broke the wireless aerial. Second officer Lloyd climbed and fixed the aerial so that an SOS message could be sent, but due to smoke inhalation 136 passengers lost their lives in a very short space of time.

Large liners arrived near the scene in response to the SOS and were standing by in the severe weather conditions. Several boats had been launched from the *Volturno*, but were instantly swamped. Edward Lloyd, though with badly burned hands and arms, volunteered to take a boat to row across the two miles of heavy seas to the German liner *Grosser Kuerferst*. He succeeded in reaching the big German liner, and later, under his direction, with the American oil tanker *Naraganset*, pouring oil on the sea, boats were put out and the passengers and crew of the ill-fated *Volturno* were taken off safely. He was definitely the hero of the hour – not only had he reactivated the damaged wireless system, but in a superb feat of seamanship, he was largely responsible for the nearly 700 survivors.

During the 1914–18 war Edward was involved in transporting troops to the Dardanelles and served for a time on the *Mauritania*. Later he served on several ships, including the *Sarastone*, running the blockade during the Spanish Civil War. He was still serving two years into the Second World War. At the end of the war he died suddenly in 1946.

Captain John Lloyd, brother of Edward Lewis, had a long and distinguished career commanding ships for Cardiff-based firms such as the Jenkins Bros. One of their ships that he commanded was the SS *St Regulus*. During World War 1, he was made Lieutenant in the RNR and was in command of Naval Transport. During his retirement, he built the house known today as Y Graig, which had its own electricity generator. Another John Lloyd (1840–1890) was mate on the schooner *Nanteos* in 1861, and on board was his younger brother David (b. 1845). John was born at Tŷ du Farm, and captained the *Florence* (1866–72), *Convoy* (1872–6) and the *Dora Ann* (1876–88), and was on the *Glenhavren* in 1890 when he died at Santiago Da Cuba. He married Mary, the daughter of Lewis Jones, master mariner, and at one time he was a major shareholder with

Borth man, William James, in the sailing vessel *Convoy*, which was eventually lost near Bahia in 1878; this ship gave her name to the house Convoy in Borth. Another relative was David Lloyd (1837–1870), who at twenty-three years old was mate on the schooner *Eleanor Francis*, and later commanded the *Naomi* (1865–1870); he drowned in an accident at Montevideo.

Another Lloyd family enterprise was the Aberdyfi-built schooner *Martha Lloyd*, which was totally Borth-owned, Captain Evan Lloyd (b. 1849) being the principal shareholder. He gained his master's certificate in 1875 and went on to command the *SS Cincora*. The *Martha Lloyd* was commanded by various Borth men including Captain William Williams (1839–1922), but was eventually wrecked off the coast of Holland.

Jim Lloyd AB spent some time at sea, after which he spent many happy hours sailing a Borth beach boat called *The Betsey*, which was later owned by Enoch Pugh and 'Jack' Ellis. In the 1930s Jim was in partnership with his cousin Edward Lewis Lloyd in the ownership of a small coaster, which traded in the Irish Sea. Unfortunately, this Borth-owned vessel was lost off the coast of the Isle of Man, luckily with no loss of life. Another relative, Oswald Lloyd of Beach Grove House, was Chief Petty Officer in the Royal Navy from 1938 until 1952, serving on *HMS Belfast* and *HMS Rapid*.

The womenfolk of the Lloyd family were also familiar with shipboard life, as the family of Edward Lewis Lloyd's wife Arina were involved in shipping affairs. Arina Lloyd and their daughter Gwen were often photographed on board ship. Arina was pictured dressed in her husband's uniform, and their daughter Gwen is seen being held aloft by her father in another photograph on board the *Principello*, of London. As a teenager, Gwen also sailed with her father on the *Sarastone* from Newport to Barry.

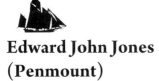

Edward John Jones (Penmount)

Edward John Jones (1878–1945) was the son of John Jones, mariner, and Jane, a laundress, of Wellington Place. After his mother died he went to live at Penmount House with his aunt Jane Thomas, his father's sister. Edward worked his way quickly up the ranks. By the age of twenty-nine he had gained his master's certificate.

Just prior to the outbreak of World War One, E. J. Jones was First Officer on the liner *Empress of Ireland*, owned by the Canadian Pacific Railways. What was to unfold was a tragedy that equalled that of the *Titanic* sinking. The liner was in collision with the Norwegian collier *Storstad* in the mouth of the St. Lawrence River. The ships had first sighted each other about ten miles apart on a calm, clear night. Adjustments were made by the captains of both vessels to ensure a safe passing. A sudden dense fog descended that caused both captains to err on the side of caution, which ironically contributed to the disaster. The captain of the *Empress of Ireland*, Henry Kendall, slowed the ship down to a crawl waiting for the other vessel to pass, before getting under way properly. Instead of passing, the *Storstad's* masthead lights materialized out of the fog heading straight toward the liner. Despite taking immediate evasive action, it was too late. As the *Storstad* was low in the water with a full cargo, and had bows especially strengthened to tackle ice that was often a hazard in the St Lawrence waterway, she cut a massive hole 25 feet long and 14 feet wide straight into the starboard side.

What followed was not helped by the fact that it was night, and most of those on the liner were asleep. Although having enough lifeboats for passengers and crew, the ship sank so swiftly that they could not be utilized. Only six boats were successfully launched; after ten minutes, the liner lurched onto her side with many passengers clinging on the slippery hull. Four minutes later she sank. The death toll was enormous: of the 1,477 souls on board, 1,012 lost their lives, including 840 passengers. In total, eight more had died than when the *Titanic* had sunk. E. J. Jones was instrumental in ensuring that as many as possible of the lifeboats got away, and desperately sought to save as many survivors as possible.

Toward the end of the Great War, he was in command of the SS *Medora*, when she was torpedoed off the coast of Ireland; this was another Canadian Pacific Railways ship. After the crew took to the lifeboats, the submarine surfaced, and in perfect English, the officer on its deck demanded that the captain, chief wireless officer and the chief gunner should be delivered to him. At first, they denied that they were aboard, but the German captain threatened to sink them on the spot if they were not delivered. Captain E. J. Jones stood up and identified himself, as he did not want to endanger the crew. The wireless operator followed suit, and a brave second gunner grabbed the chief gunner's hat and stood up, as he knew that the chief gunner was a married man with children. After the three men had been taken aboard the submarine, it commenced firing again, until the *Medora* sunk.

Shortly after this incident, another ship reported that she had destroyed a German submarine in the area, and there was a great fear that the *Medora* prisoners had gone down with that submarine. However, soon after the British were notified that the three were safely landed and were in a prison camp. Captain Jones survived his ordeal and returned to work for the Canadian company. He was captain of the *Empress of Australia* in 1941. He was awarded an OBE for services during the Second World War. He retired from the sea in 1942, and died three years later.

The Jones Family
(Emmett and Tŷ Mawr)

There were other Jones mariners who may have been related to the five or so Jones families previously profiled. Captain John Jones of the sloop *Linnet* was active in the 1760s, and later ran the sloop *Neptune* in 1820. A close relative of his, Morgan Jones, also ran the sloop *Linnet* in 1826. Lewis Jones (1796–1860) was captain of the *Emmett*. Captain John Jones (b. 1821) commanded his own schooner the *Jane Jones* for fifteen years. Another John Jones (b. 1825) was master of the *Panthea* and the barque *Hawarden Castle*, on which he died at Calcutta. David Jones (b. 1835) was master of the *Abbey* for several years. John Jones (b. 1838) was master of the *Swallow* and lived at Tŷ Mawr. He gave navigation lessons in the latter half of his career. Captain David Jones (1842-80) commanded the sailing vessels *Forest Prince* and the *Adeliza*, a vessel on which he died. Yet another John Jones (b. 1863) was master of the steamers *Graffoe, Collingham, Armenia, Usher* and the *Charles Tellier*.

John Leslie Matthews

John Leslie Matthews was born in 1902, and educated at Morfa Borth Primary School, and then Machynlleth Secondary School. He left school at fourteen and first went to sea on the same ship as his Uncle 'Harry' Henry Levi Williams, his mother's brother. This first trip was to America in 1916. This was a very dangerous time to begin seafaring, and like others from Borth, he was to fall victim to a sinking. At only fifteen, he found himself in the lifeboat after the *SS Huntsholm*, captained by John Davies of Borth, had been torpedoed. The survivors were given a position to steer to the nearest landfall by the U-boat captain. This was quite an experience: there was a constant fear that survivors would be machine-gunned.

After the First World War John Leslie served on ships owned by J. J. Denholm of Glasgow: the *SS Broompark*, as an ordinary seaman, and then the *SS Beechpark* as an able seaman. Again, he voyaged under Captain John Davies, who eventually went from Borth to Bow Street to retire. In 1924, John Leslie was on the *SS Plas Dinam*, a vessel once owned and commanded by Captain John Davies of Maesteg. His next vessel was the *SS Councillor*.

At the age of twenty-four, John Leslie went to Cleaves Nautical School in Liverpool, to sit for his second mate's certificate. He passed at the end of 1926. He joined the *SS Laurelpark* as second officer, and served on her for a number of years. He gained his first mate's certificate at Liverpool in 1928. The following year, he was on the *SS Navarino* as a second officer, and in 1930, he was on the *SS Knight of Saint George*, owned by Pardoe & Thomas Co. Newport, Monmouthshire as third officer. As his promotions were increasing, his employment positions were decreasing, as shipping economies were already feeling the pinch of the Great Depression. This vessel was to be his last for a time, and it sailed from Penarth with coal to Monte Video and Santa Fe, a port 200 miles up the River Plate. The return cargo was grain.

By 1931, having tried for many positions with innumerable

companies, he was unable to find maritime employment. Many of his letters and replies from this time are held by his son John. In the end, he accepted a job from a cousin of his grandmother's to manage a small livestock food factory in Surrey. There he met his wife, and despite the Depression, they managed to live a relatively comfortable life. All was well until the Second World War broke out. The owner of the factory died, causing the company to be closed down.

Leslie took his wife back to his home village of Borth and they decided to stay there for a while. With the war beginning in earnest, and Leslie at a bit of a loose end, he decided to approach the local recruiting officer, who promised to fix him up with a job in air-sea rescue boats. He joined up at the beginning of 1941, presuming that he would be based in the UK, where the theatre of his activities would be the Western Approaches. However, the RAF decided a qualified Merchant Navy officer would be better deployed in the jungles of Asia. This infuriated his wife, as amongst other things Leslie was by now forty years old. After training he was sent out to India by troopship, and eventually to Burma, where he spent an uncomfortable war tracking Japanese planes from small trucks in the energy-sapping humidity, relaying details back to base. He was 'demobbed' in late 1945, returning to Borth to take over the family butcher's shop after his father became seriously ill.

John L. Matthew's mother's brother, Uncle 'Harry', Henry Levi Williams, was a beloved rascal of the family. He was named after his father Levi, and uncle, Henry, who were both seafarers. Once when home from sea, nothing would do but he had to help out at the butcher's shop by delivering meat in the horse and trap. All was going well until he dented the wing of a summer visitor's car. The hot and bothered car owner cursed the 'Welsh peasant' to such a degree that the normally placid Harry decided not to apologize. Instead, he jumped out of the trap and kicked dents in the other wing, and with a terse farewell said, 'There you are, even a peasant like me has matched it up,' and trotted off in his horse and cart.

Harry had quite a chequered career. He once jumped ship in Newfoundland and stayed there for a number of years. He saw active service in the Boer War and the Great War. In the 1914–18 conflict, he was second officer on the *SS Hillglade* when she was chased by the German battle cruiser *Dresden* in the Straits of Magellan, but managed to escape in a blizzard. Later he was on the SS *Cheltonian* with Captain Enos when it was sunk in the Mediterranean. Harry and other crew-members drifted for several days in an open boat before landing safely in France.

Danger lurked again as he found himself having to be rescued by a British destroyer when his vessel the *Usher* sank on escort duty. In the 1930s, he often ran the Bilbao Blockade on the SS *Stanhope*. Harry worked for many years for the Denholm Company Glasgow, and often found berths for many Borth lads and appears with them in several photographs.

Henry Levi Williams (1869–1938), who survived the Boer War and First World War, only to die in a bombing raid during the Spanish Civil War

Harry's reckless nature caught up with him in the end at fifty-nine years old. In June 1938 at Cartagena during the Spanish Civil War, despite warnings not to go ashore as the city was a possible target for bomber planes owing to the nearby military base, off Harry went to town. At this time, he was third mate on the *Stanholm*, which also had another Borth man, Evan Leslie Davies, of Mona House, as first officer. As fate would have it, there was a raid on the town. Harry was the only fatality from the crew.

The Williams Family (Epworth and Francon)

The Williams family had a long association with the Aberystwyth vessel the *Ocean Belle*, with three brothers, Levi, Henry and Richard, and a cousin, John, all sailing on her. The Borth connection initially began with Captain William James (1820–1880), who commanded her from 1859 to 1863, with his nephew, John Williams (b. 1835), as first mate. Captain James had previously commanded the *Aberystwyth* and the *Island Maid*, then the *Ocean Belle* and *Dorothy* before going to live at Aberdyfi after retiring from the sea to concentrate on ship ownership. He bought the small 588-ton barque *Glendovey* in 1876, and put John Williams, by then aged forty, in charge of her. John had become captain in 1862, and took command of the *Ocean Belle* and then from 1867 until 1869, the *Dorothy*. He then sailed the *Glendovey* worldwide for a period of twenty-four years, until his retirement at the age of sixty in 1900. His father, Evan, had been mate on the 62-ton schooner *Virtue* of Newport in 1845.

Captain Levi Williams (b. 1840) sailed as first mate on the *Ocean Belle* for a decade, as had his cousin John before him, both under the command of William James. Levi gained his master's certificate in 1877, and later captained the *Pilgrim*. His brother, Henry (b. 1838) was mate on the *Picton*, and in 1871, whilst mate on the schooner *Jane Jones*, took his wife Mary Ann with him. Henry is buried in Phillipville, Algeria. Another brother, Captain Richard Williams (1843-99) commanded and eventually owned the 170-ton *Ocean Belle* from 1875 until 1899. He had previously served as mate on this vessel and on its last ill-fated voyage, his nephew John Whitlock Williams (1868-99), son of Henry and Mary Ann, was serving as first mate. The vessel foundered in December 1899 off the coast of Denmark, near Lemvig. The tragedy is described thus: 'A vessel came in sight last evening, in a south-west direction, burning a flash light. About one hour later, the light disappeared and shortly afterwards some wreckage and two lifebuoys marked *Ocean Belle* of

Aberystwyth came ashore'. The vessel was concluded to have sunk with all hands. Several bodies were recovered, among whom was Captain Williams, who left a wife, one daughter and four sons.

The name Whitlock first appears with a Whitlock Williams, master mariner, who died in 1840; his wife was Margaret (neé Jones). They had married in Llandre in the 1790s. Both were probably from Borth, but had moved to Aberystwyth. Margaret had a nephew born a year after her husband died, so in remembrance he was named John Whitlock Jones (1841-66); he died of cholera at twenty-five years old in Calcutta whilst serving as mate on the *City of Sydney*. There was John Whitlock Williams (1841-79), another master mariner, who died at sea aged thirty-eight, and his wife Margaret (1839-87), both buried in Llandre churchyard.

William Thomas Williams, a shareholder in the *Ocean Belle*, was one of Captain Richard Williams' sons, who lived at Aberystwyth. Captain Richard Williams' daughter, Margaret, married Captain John H. Roberts of Borth y Gest, and they lived for a time at Gordon Villa, before moving to Liverpool. In 1916, Captain Roberts was in command of the *Lestris* on a voyage from Liverpool to Rotterdam, when she was captured and towed to Zeebrugge. They were the parents of Captain Richard William Roberts OBE (b. 1901), who had a glittering maritime career.

Another son, Thomas Williams (1874–1945), was a master mariner who built Francon House on Cliff Road and commanded the SS *Kentish Coast* in World War One, receiving a commendation from the Admiralty and the Ministry of shipping. He voyaged innumerable times, without mishap, to South America during the First World War, bringing back horses for the army on the Western Front, and vital cargoes of meat; all this being carried out whilst the U-boat attacks intensified. His sister-in-law married John Brodigan (1881–1959), who often sailed with Captain Williams as bosun, as did my grandfather. There were other Brodigan relatives who were mariners living in Aberystwyth. Captain Thomas Williams had a master mariner son, Henry Whitlock Williams (1908-50), who also had a distinguished career. He became master in 1939 and commanded the *Hartismere, Harpalion* and *Hartington*. The *Harpalion* was sunk in 1942 by enemy fire. The captain, like his father before him, was highly commended for his war service.

The Davies Family (Bodina)

As previously mentioned, John L. Matthews often sailed with Captain John Davies (1877–1937), whose wife Mary Jane neé Thomas (1876–1967) came from Bow Street. Captain Davies gained his master's certificate in 1897, and during the next thirty years commanded many ships, including the steamers *King David, King Cadwallon, King Edward, King Gruffydd, Huntsholme, Broompark, Beechpark* and the *Lylepark*. The latter vessel he took on her maiden voyage after being guest of honour at her launching, where he was presented with a commemorative book entitled *Two Centuries of Shipbuilding*, a history of the company that built the Lylepark at Greenock.

Captain John Davies, Bodina, commended in 1906 for his humanitarian intervention in a pogrom against Ukranian Jews

In June 1906 Captain Davies was in the Black Sea in command of the *SS King Edward* at a time when there was a pogrom taking place against the Jews. The ship docked at Cherson, which is near Odessa, and upon seeing the plight of the Jewish people he decided that he had to provide sanctuary for them. About 100 people were ushered safely aboard his ship. For this humanitarian act he received a written testament and a silver commemorative cup from the Jewish community. Part of the testament reads as follows: 'You acted in a most humane and kind way and showed your love of your fellow men. In this you behaved with the highest act of humanity'.

His generous nature was again evident when he bought the house Ivanhoe, now called Tŷ Canol, from Captain Hughes so that his parents Evan (1841–1924) and Margaret (1849–1934), and also his spinster sister Margaret, could live there, whilst he himself went to live in Bodina House, Bow Street. This house was named after his eldest daughter Ina; it translates from the Welsh as meaning 'Ina's Dwelling'. He was another captain who took his wife with him on his voyages. This was facilitated by Ina, capably looking after her siblings during her parents' absence at sea.

The captain had two sons (one of whom, Marcus, died as a child) and three daughters. His surviving son Thomas Whitlock Davies (1907-47) completed a five-year engineering apprenticeship before becoming a ship's engineer on Denholm Line vessels. He then bought a garage in Aberaeron, a venture encouraged by his uncle, Captain Evan Williams (1876–1958) of Borth, who had married an Aberaeron girl and lived at Bodryddan, her family home in North Road. He was captain of the *Ardgowan* (1913–1930); renamed *Mesopotamia* in 1916. In his old age he often stayed for the summer with his relatives at Francon House, Borth. Thomas Whitlock Davies and his young family moved to Aberaeron to run his new business venture. Sadly, within a few years he had died of cancer. From that time, Captain Williams became a sort of surrogate father to the three children, and no doubt encouraged them to take up a maritime career.

John Whitlock Davies (b. 1939) worked as a ship's engineer for the Elder Dempster Lines on the motor vessels, *Fourah Bay, Dunkwa, Sulima, Falaba, Fulani* and *Ebani*. His brother, Thomas Malcolm Davies (b. 1936) served on over forty Shell Tankers including *Partula, Hyala, Hadra, Mangelia, Harpula, Opalia, Lima, Halia* and *Serenia*.

Captain Davies' daughter Ina had a son Marcus Whitlock Evans (1936-98), who became a ship's engineer after serving an apprenticeship with Cammel Laird of Birkenhead. Another daughter, Nesta, who married a Richards, had a son Michael who became a ship's engineer, and now lives in Penegoes. Instead of doing a five-year shore-based engineering apprenticeship like his relatives, he undertook a four-and-a- half-year apprenticeship, which involved two years at college, six months work experience, six months back at college followed by eighteen months at sea. From 1960 to 1990 he worked for British Petroleum, and was on many ships including the *British Renown, British Ranger, British Explorer, British Tay* and the *British Trent*. Michael remembers coming to Borth to consult with retired ship's engineer Joe Rees of Gordon Villa about his future career. It is quite remarkable that five descendants of master mariner John Davies all became ship's engineers.

John Matthews

At sixteen years old John Matthews (b. 1940) decided to follow in his father J. Leslie Matthews' footsteps, and join the Merchant Navy. He signed indentures for four years as an apprentice with Reardon Smith & Co. Ltd, the well-known Cardiff deep sea tramping company. By the time he was eighteen he had steamed around the world twice, calling at many ports with a lot of water in between. The ships that John was on were mostly built during World War Two and were not expected to last, but many of them did. Food was never brilliant, but the apprentices' accommodation was acceptable as they had their own cabins with bunk, desk, wardrobe and settee on the boat deck.

The ships John served on carried mostly bulk cargoes – coal, iron ore, grain, salt, phosphate and soya beans. He rarely knew how long a trip would last as cargoes were often negotiated whilst the ship was at sea. The longest trip John did was just over twelve months. The company ships averaged 7,000 gross tons were 400 feet long with an average speed of 10 knots.

John's first trip was on the *MV Orient City*, sailing from Cardiff to Brazil to pick up a cargo of iron ore for the UK. In November of 1956 he joined the *MV Cornish City* in Barry, which was preparing to take army stores to Egypt as the Suez crisis was still on. However, things quickly settled, so instead the vessel sailed to New Orleans to pick up a load of soya beans heading for Japan via the Panama Canal. After a five-week haul across the Pacific, the cargo was discharged at Kobe. John remembers Japan in those days as a great place for seamen and a real eye-opener for a boy from Borth. Then it was down to West Australia to load grain for the UK, and home via the Cape of Good Hope, calling in at Cape Town and Dakkar in Senegal. John stayed on this vessel for nearly two years.

His next vessel was the *MV Homer City*, which had an all-Indian crew with British officers and apprentices. This was the best 'feeder' as its cook was a real chef who had at one time worked in the best hotels in Calcutta. John developed a taste for curry on this vessel and has fond memories of some wonderful meals. The next vessel was *MV Vancouver City*, on which he stayed until his indentures expired and he was eventually paid off a few days short of his twenty-first birthday in 1961. Although he enjoyed his time at sea, and never regretted it, he decided it was not something he wanted to do for the rest of his life, so he called it a day and stayed ashore.

He recalls that the whole idea about being an officer was that you would be able to do any job on board ship, therefore any orders you would give you would be capable of doing yourself, no matter how hazardous. During rough weather he used to manoeuvre his mattress to wedge himself in, but with a storm lasting days, this could be especially wearing. The worst event he remembers was a typhoon while in port at Japan. After the warning came, the ship took off out to sea to ride it out. Both anchors were put down with the bow facing into the wind and the engine turning over slowly to take the strain. The force of the wind was frightening and John wondered if he would ever see Borth again. The vessel survived and on returning to port they could see the devastation that had taken place. Strangely enough, this vessel, the *Vancouver City*, was later driven ashore in a typhoon off Japan and had to be scrapped.

One of John's abiding memories was picking up a cargo of coal from Virginia, which meant sailing up Chesapeake Bay where a large naval review was taking place. This involved warships from all over the world and included some beautiful sail-training ships. Whilst steaming through this spectacle, John was told to dip the ensign out of courtesy. In turn it was amazing to see these wonderful vessels, some with their crews lined up on deck, responding by saluting John's vessel, a rusty old tramp from Cardiff. By a strange coincidence, a short time later, another tramp steamer passed, and John spotted Borth lad, John 'Jac' Evans, on its deck. A year later they met up at home and confirmed this fact.

Raymond Hughes

Raymond Hughes, the son of Richard David and Elizabeth Hughes, attended Towyn School as a boarder, but as soon as he was sixteen he was off to sea. He was from seafaring stock. One of his father's brothers William, jumped ship in 1912 and lived all his life in New Zealand. Yet Raymond's father, very much against family tradition, joined the army. He was initially in a Scottish regiment, and then joined the Royal Horse Artillery, where apparently he was on the leading gun carriage that entered Jerusalem after the Turks were driven out of Palestine in the First World War. As village lore put it, 'He was one of the first Christians to enter that city since the last crusade'.

Raymond, in his first year as deck boy, went on three voyages, two on the *Dallas City* and on his last fatal voyage, the *SS Bradfyne*. On the latter ship Evan William Lewis, who was married to Raymond's Auntie Mary, was the bosun, so it was natural that Raymond would join his uncle. In November of 1940 the *Bradfyne*, a Reardon Smith Line vessel, was sunk by the German submarine U100, south of Rockall. The two Borth men and thirty-six others lost their lives; only four men survived. By a strange quirk Raymond's previous vessel the *Dallas City*, was bombed and sunk by German planes in the same year. Raymond was only sixteen at the time, and his Uncle Evan forty-six. Evan had already lost his brother to a German U-boat twenty-two years earlier.

Raymond's sister Eileen remembers the fateful day when the telegram arrived. All she recalls was an ominous silence that had descended on the house, and unexpectedly being taken by the postman back to his family where she spent the day. Other than the one remaining photograph, she cannot remember her brother as she was only three at the time. Eileen often ponders over this tragedy and how stoic her parents must have been, as her father suffered from shell shock, the outcome of his service in the First World War. Eileen is married to John Davies, a descendant of the Ffosygravel mariners and those of Llanon.

Hugh Hughes
(Boston House)

One of the major influences on young John Matthews was Hugh David Hughes (1927-2006). Hugh lived opposite John in Boston House, and was known to everyone as 'Hugh Boston'. John Matthews remembers Hugh bringing him American comics every time he came home on leave. They were rare and welcome items for a young boy in the 1940s. Hugh was from a family of seafarers who were related to many other Borth families; his grandfather, David Hughes, had captained the *SS Eira* and relatives were often crew-members. Some of them lost their lives when that ship disappeared on a voyage to Kronstadt in 1898. Hugh is summed up in the following extract from a reference given prior to his going to sea: 'Seventeen years old, good education, tall and of a smart appearance.

Hugh David Hughes,
known in Borth as 'Hugh Boston'

He is honest, trustworthy and of an excellent character that is beyond reproach. Very nice young man and good natured'.

Hugh's early years were somewhat blighted as he had tuberculosis, which meant that he spent two years convalescing away from home at Llandrindod Wells at a sanitorium grandly named Highland Moors. He recalled listening to the news about the sinking of the *Graf Spee*.

At sea, he began by working his way up the promotion ladder from being a deck hand. He was an AB by 1953 and by 1955 he had obtained his second mate's certificate. Hugh served on the *Angelo* of Hull, *Seaboard Enterprise* of Barry and as third mate on the great ocean liner *Queen Elizabeth*, voyaging to Canada and Australia. On one of his voyages to the Antipodes, a block broke loose and fell just as Hugh was passing. He suffered a severe head injury, which resulted in him being hospitalized for two months in Australia.

It was so difficult for him to find a ship to return on that he seriously thought of taking out citizenship – not only because he liked the country, but so that he could get a position on an Australian ship to get back home. Luckily he found a ship and came back to the UK. His last years at sea were again on the *Queen Elizabeth*, which he enjoyed immensely.

During one trip across the North Atlantic in winter on an overcast day, he arrived on the bridge where it became evident that something unusual was afoot. The knowing demeanour of the other officers, and a strange aura of silence and stillness seemed to have descended upon the ship. Hugh eventually broke the silence asking what was up, and was there anything wrong? They all pointed to the starboard side. Hugh looked at the dark sea and the light-coloured sky above it. Suddenly he looked again and realized that the sky was actually a mountainous iceberg. As he said, 'It was both beautiful and sinister'.

Hugh crossed the Atlantic many times and became quite familiar with New York. Being generous to a fault, like his father, D. H. Hughes (David 'Boston'), before him, he always bought presents back: scent for his mother and sister, and comics and magazines for neighbouring youngsters. David 'Boston' had been a stretcher-bearer in World War One. He almost single-handedly bankrupted Boston Stores as he would freely give credit. Unfortunately, a stomach infection meant Hugh had to leave the sea as he knew from past experience that it could be risky to fall ill on board ship. By 1958 he was ashore and a member of the Aberystwyth Fire Brigade. There he met his wife Verona, and they settled down to live in Aberystwyth. He was involved with many activities to do with young people, and despite advancing years and ill health he still refereed local football matches. As his wife Verona recalls, even in his last days when he was in hospital, he insisted that she fill in his referee registration forms for the following year.

Ships' Engineers

Hugh Hughes' uncle, Joseph Rees, was a ship's engineer and was one of many from Borth including John Thomas Richards, Thomas Lloyd, David Jenkins, John Lewis, Enoch Davies, David Rees, George Meddins, John B. Lewis, Thomas Arter, W. Llewelyn Arter, Daniel Evan Jones, James Daniel and Owen Robert Hughes.

John and Gethin Evans

John 'Jac' Evans (b. 1936) and his older brother Gethin (b. 1943), of Deudraeth House, both went to sea. I remember Gethin Evans arriving at Soar Chapel in his RAF uniform on a long-ago Sunday. It caused a welcome distraction as Raymond Cousins, Thomas Glyn Evans and I were trying desperately to read a verse, supposedly learnt by heart, from the Bible through the communion wine hole in front of our pew. I think our long-suffering Sunday school teacher, Mr. Jones of Preswylfa House, had realized our weekly verse-reading was too flawless to be genuine, and also done with suspiciously unchar-acteristic piety, as our foreheads were pressed against the front of the pew. Gethin was receiving a copy of the New Testament, a gift from the chapel elders, to take with him on his National Service stint. He served in Germany with the RAF regiment for two years before returning to finish an apprenticeship as a carpenter with his uncle's firm Dole Builders. Soon after the sea proved too much of a lure and he decided to train as a wireless operator.

He went to sea on tankers for four years, and enjoyed the life, but marriage was beckoning. At the same time a potentially life-threatening incident occurred whilst he was off the coast of Canada, when he developed a severe case of appendicitis. He was winched up into a helicopter and taken to hospital in Nova Scotia. He underwent an emergency operation, and after convalescing he came home. It had been a close shave, and if it had occurred in mid Atlantic, he would have been in serious trouble. Gethin settled back in Borth to raise a family and run a building business and became involved in village life as a councillor and Lord Mayor. He, with Aran Morris, was instrumental in bringing the lifeboat to Borth.

Jac Evans was in the sea cadets at Aberystwyth whilst still at school. He was invited to represent the cadets at a review on *HMS Dido*, and for a time seriously considered a career in the Royal Navy. However he was advised by the old seamen of Borth to join the Merchant Navy: at least he could leave it if he did not like it, unlike the Royal Navy. Jac went to the Merchant Navy Training School Vindicatrix. He was at one time one of the youngest ABs in the Swansea pool. Jac is often mentioned in the memoirs of his one time shipmate, the late Gerry Evans of Aberystwyth, who went to live in New Zealand. As I worked with Jac for a time for his brother's building company, I heard many a yarn, some far too outrageous to print. Jac had sailed just at the end of the era of tramping steamers and had been to literally hundreds of ports all over the world. Some of the vessels he sailed on were the *Kenuta, Loch Ryan* and the *Dashwood*. I always remember him as a genuine, fun-loving, kindhearted person, with never a bad word to say about anybody.

After a day's work, either on the building site, or his brother Gethin's fishing boat, Jac and I would go for a few drinks at the Friendship Inn. Nothing would do but we had to go dragnetting, which was only occasionally fruitful. By 2 a.m. we would be back at his mother's house for a fry up of whatever fish had been caught.

At one time Jac joined the *Kenuta,* a cargo/passenger vessel belonging to the Pacific Steam Navigation Company in London. After calling at Liverpool she was bound for the west coast of America. It was the start of a long adventurous trip, as no sooner had the vessel came up to St George's Channel, than it was enveloped in a dense fog. Jac was at the wheel when suddenly he heard a great commotion and shouting, and suddenly the officer on duty ordered the vessel to stop so that they could launch a lifeboat, as they had just run down a French trawler. Thankfully, all eight fishermen were rescued and taken aboard to be landed at Liverpool. Jac remembered all the Frenchmen cursing every hour until they reached Liverpool. He found it sobering that no-one, including himself, felt any impact when the vessel cut the trawler in half.

After leaving Liverpool they crossed the Atlantic and went through the Panama Canal and then on to Buenaventura in Colombia. Jac remembered it as a young sailor's heaven, cheap booze and beautiful women everywhere. Eventually they reached Antofagasta in Chile, and taking time out there, Jac and shipmate Gerry Evans teamed up with a couple of South American girls who took them back to their flat. There they enjoyed some wonderful food, which was a change from the meals they were served on the ship. The *Kenuta* was leaving at midnight, but Jac was in seventh heaven and the party in full swing; they forgot all about their ship, which sailed without them.

The next morning they rushed down hoping to get a bus to Valparaiso to catch up with the ship. There was a nasty surprise waiting. The captain had left word with the authorities to put them in jail until the ship returned in two weeks' time. They were given a camp bed to sleep on. Prisoners such as themselves were provided with meals. The shipping companies would be billed and the sailors' wages docked accordingly when they got home. Being a country where wine was cheap, this was provided two or three times a day. As Jac recalled, they were quietly living like kings.

By chance, some young detectives attached to the police station, who had been on training courses in the USA, decided to come and practice their English, which resulted in a great friendship developing. This two-week-long siesta came to an abrupt end with the return of the *Kenuta*. Jac was hauled up before the captain, and he was duly told how much of his wages were going to be docked. Towards evening of that day, a message arrived that the police wanted to see Jac and his shipmate again. There was a great deal of smirking from the captain and the first mate, thinking that they were going to give Jac a bit of a pasting just to remind him of his misdemeanours in Chile. However, it was the detective friends, who took them on another nights' bender round the town. Jac almost compounded his errant ways by missing the ship again. It seemed that Jac was forever in one scrape or another.

Eventually, he married Ann, an Aberystwyth girl, and settled down to a shore life. He was in the fire brigade for a time and then went to work for his brother's building company. Eventually he struck out on his own and was a builder based at Aberystwyth. I last saw him a month before he suddenly died. We had arranged a night out on the town, which sadly did not happen. I attended his funeral, and I will never forget the words of the minister who had known Jac for a long time when he said at the end of the service that 'Jac was now going on his last voyage'. He was a much-loved person and I and many others of his friends miss him greatly.

Aran Morris

As a young man, Aran Morris (b. 1918) worked with his father, Thomas Rowley Morris, at the small grocery shop fronting Belair house. T. R. Morris had been in the Merchant Navy as well as serving in the RNVR on minesweepers in World War One. Aran's uncles did not pursue a seafaring career. Douglas became a professional golfer and George a vicar. Thomas' father had been a tanner at Factory Forge on the banks of the Afon Leri, between Dolybont and Talybont.

Aran attended Ardwyn Grammar School. After leaving school he decided he would take up engineering and went to Birmingham to work. At this time, war clouds were gathering. It was an unsettling time. He hated the confining nature of his job and told his father that he was coming back to Borth. His father suggested he take over the shop and the premises. For a time Aran was involved in local coastguard work in the Borth area. He was approaching twenty years old, and with a war about to commence he decided to volunteer. He chose the Royal Navy as he thought the army was too risky and so was the air force. His initial training was at Skegness, which he remembered as a cold icy place, where conditions were so bad that winter that one of the

Aran Morris (b. 1918), who served in Arctic convoys in the Second World War

trainees died in his bed.

His introduction to the 'proper' war was quite a shock for him. He was put on a train down to Ramsgate where he joined a large group of naval men sleeping on the dance floor of a very large hotel. He was rudely awakened at 5.am. and he and three others were placed on a 25-foot pleasure boat called the *Barnham Nostrum*, skippered by its civilian owner. He was not sure quite what was going on and as he recalls when they passed the Goodwin buoys, often mentioned by his seafaring father, the thought struck him that he was a long way from land. When a pall of smoke was seen on the horizon, the reality of the mission to evacuate the troops at Dunkirk came home to him. At first he took the low-flying aircraft as being a protective RAF but he was told in no uncertain terms that they were German planes. Soon whistling bombs were landing everywhere. They picked up a dozen men and hastened back to Ramsgate on this the last day of the evacuation.

After this he joined *HMS Columbo*, which was an epic itself. He and other crew-members were shipped out to Capetown and then journeyed by train to Durban, which took three days; needless to say the town was drunk dry on the first day. He saw quite a bit of south east Africa on this journey.

Aran arrived in Mombasa on the *Kadine Ismail* to join *HMS Columbo*. He then went on an exotic tour of the Indian Ocean, visiting Mogadishu and the Maldives. During this tropical voyage comfort parcels from home arrived full of inappropriate scarves, mufflers and balaclavas! Back in Plymouth he joined the *HMS Onslaught*, which in its final stages of being built. His idyll was soon to change into real war as he spent the majority of his service days on the Russian convoys.

The commander was Joe Selby from Gloucester, who continually won the first prize for telling the filthiest stories on board ship. Aran recalls:

If I had been cold before at Skegness, it was tropical compared to the atrocious weather on voyages to Russia as sub-zero temperatures and gale force winds continued unabated. Our decks were covered with snow and ice, and of course the danger of bombers and submarines was constant. The crew was advised not to wash as the natural body oils would help against the cold, especially when they had to go on deck and axe off the ice from the armaments. There were to be no hammocks used as they were a fire hazard. We were on constant alert, so we had to sleep where we could, and at times this meant sharing sleeping quarters with dead bodies, both German and British'.

As the official history of the Arctic convoys show, there were terrible losses; three quarters of one convoy were lost in less than half an hour. On one occasion the German battleship *Ulm* was sunk and the *HMS Onslaught* took aboard the survivors. Mess tables were being used to perform surgery, and another Welsh rating, holding an amputated arm, enquired what he should do with it. The immediate reply was 'throw it overboard'. Many surgical procedures were performed without anaesthetic.

With all the lives lost and the outstanding courage displayed one would have expected a rapturous welcome by the Russians; however, this was not to be. Aran recalls that part of their cargo included a complete field operating theatre and trained staff to go with it. Although help was offered it was refused point blank as the Russians thought that the medical staff were spies. The docks at Murmansk were piled high with supplies yet the convoy crew's rations were miniscule. All in all Russia was hardly a welcoming place. Being on the convoys for over two years meant that at times it was continual night, and as Aran recalls, 'At other times you could read comics at midnight'.

After the Russian convoys, *HMS Onslaught* became involved with the Normandy landings. Aran remembers that the conditions were so bad, with many of the invasion forces being shot to pieces, that the thought crossed his mind that his luck would run out, so he ate four bars of chocolate that he had been saving up, thinking it would be his last meal. Instead he was sick for two days, which probably helped take his mind off things. Even though the *Onslaught* was hit a number of times, there were no casualties.

As his duties had seen him involved with signals and assisting with navigation it was suggested that with his seagoing experience he might apply for a commission and stay on for a naval career. He refused this and left the ship at Portsmouth. The next thing he found that he was on the *HMS Black Swan*, which was sent to the war in the Pacific. By the time he got there the atom bomb had been dropped and Japan had surrendered. Most of the time was spent going round the Pacific repatriating Japanese units, many of whom had not realised the war was over.

Aran returned to Plymouth to be discharged, and dressed up in his 'demob' suit returned home to run the family business. He has unfailingly served the Borth community in many capacities. He was instrumental in bringing the lifeboat to Borth, as was Gethin Evans. Recently Aran has been awarded an MBE, a long overdue recognition of his services to the community.

Alan Morris

Alan Morris, Aran's son, went to sea as an apprentice officer with the British Petroleum Company. On 6 November 1968, after playing golf on Borth beach with friends, on one of those unusually sunny days in late autumn, he went home to Bel-air. After lunch with his parents, Alan put on his uniform and walked over to Gleanor to say farewell to his grandparents. This must have been quite a poignant moment for them as three decades earlier they had farewelled their son Aran, also on his way to sea. Alan remembers walking down to the station with his father in the company of Nick Brown and ex-mariner Gethin Evans. As Nick and his father were giving him serious advice, Gethin, trying to lighten the occasion, kept interspersing the conversation with lurid tales of life as a sailor.

There was no training school course so he went straight to Sinnart, West Scotland, to join the tanker *British Destiny*. His introduction to life at sea was to haul up a gyrocompass all the way from the dock to the bridge. The ship left that night and ran into a fierce storm where upon he became as sick as a dog. As he passed roughly where he thought Borth was he mused that a lifeboat rescue from there would do just fine at this time. This first trip was from the UK to the Persian Gulf and on to Australia; back to the Persian Gulf then Australia again and finally back to North Shields. He then managed three days at home as the vessel was in dry dock for her fifteen-year survey.

The next ship was the tanker *British Poplar*, where each trip was six months long. The ship carried three apprentices, whose duties included cleaning sludge from the bilges, obviously, as Alan said, tongue in cheek, 'to build moral fibre in future officers'.

Alan took his steering ticket after innumerable hours at the wheel, initially, of course, far out to sea, to cope with yawing and the like. After a while he was good enough to be allowed to take the vessel in and out of port. He says he was a gibbering wreck when he completed the arrival. During his time with BP he was on the *British*

Argosy, British Flag and *British Valour*. Later on, after joining the Scottish Management Company, Glasgow, he sailed on the *Cape Leeuwin, Temple Bar, Cape Wrath* and the *Baron Dunmore*.

Alan was involved in developing one of the world's first automated container terminals. Currently, even with the new fully automated unloading facilities at Brisbane, Australia, there are still certain types of stevedoring jobs. New skills being developed give the lie to the term 'fully automated', and as he says, 'some aspects of stevedoring are nowadays totally obsolete, but others are quite new and therefore they create a job market'. Alan has sailed as cargo superintendent on twenty or so ships. Nowadays he still manages the odd trip in that capacity, although his current position keeps him at the port of Brisbane for most of the time. It is noticeable how deeply affected he still is by *hiraeth* for his home place, Borth.

Len and Stephen Dennett

Len Dennett, born in Kent in 1920, had an affinity with the Welsh, as most of his school chums were the sons of Welsh miners working in the Kent coalfields. He trained as a chef then got a position on a private yacht, the *Davydon*. In 1939 he was on this vessel on a canal near Calais in France. There was short delay prior to crossing back to England because of the outbreak of the war. On 14 November 1939 he joined *HMS Hergar*, reg. 161241, on a T124 admiralty agreement. This vessel acted as escort for the east coast fishing fleet from Grimsby to Yarmouth and also did boom defense work. Len was paid off after this vessel was in a collision with the minelayer *HMS Salamander.*

On 7 May 1940 he joined the *HMV Camroux*, a coaster, which had been seconded by the RAF for experimental work involving night drifting toward German minefields off the French coast for the purpose of fine-tuning radar systems. There was also some connection with the balloon establishment at Cardington.

In August 1940 the vessel was sent to Fishguard and spent most of its time voyaging along the Welsh coastline. It began working with the Aberporth rocket range by positioning targets in Cardigan Bay. The vessel had been to Heysham to pick up large-scale models of bombers, which were hung from huge balloons anchored out from Aberporth. They were part of the experiments with rockets which dispersed hundreds of little parachutes, which trailed wires meant to foul airplane propellers. Len remembers that on occasion some of these weird and wonderful experiments would go awry as rockets would home in on the ship itself so it was full speed ahead. The *Camroux* would pick up various types of rockets and ammunition from an arsenal at Trecwn, Pembrokeshire, and often lay targets offshore from Manorbier and Pendine Sands. When based later at Aberdyfi he frequently saw sailing cutters full of young trainee officers from the Outward Bound School at that port. Len felt sorry for them as they were often out at sea for three or four days and looked totally worn out by the experience.

In 1942, the RAF personnel left the *Camroux* to be replaced by some thirty army officers and men to be taken to Aberdyfi. They lived on board ship whilst the Ynyslas camp was being completed. Effectively the vessel had switched from RAF control to Royal Ordnance control and was from then on based at Aberdyfi. Len recalls, 'The army needed us to mark the low-water line all around the Dyfi. The vast estuarine area within it they squared off into grids, each of which was a target area for the rockets being fired from the Ynyslas base. We also fired a few rockets and shells at various times. Our vessel was essentially a coaster that had been cleared and armed for the special work we were to do. The idea of the target grids was to ensure accuracy of the weapons they were experimenting with.'

In 1943 when Barnes Wallace was experimenting with what was later to become the dambuster bomb, part of the tests took place at a lake near Capel Curig. Scientists and army personnel were billeted in a large hall near the area and as there were no ATS women available to do the cooking Len was sent up there to cater for them. 'All I remember was that it was winter time and freezing cold up there.'

In essence the *Camroux*, whilst based in Aberdyfi, was working for the Royal Ordnance Company developing and testing rockets, projectiles, radio, radar and underwater propulsions at Ynyslas and Borth. What Len finds perplexing is the apparent ignorance about what went on at Ynyslas and its important contribution to the war effort. There are no accounts, personal or otherwise, and certainly no evidence in local museums.

At the end of the war, the *Camroux* was quickly converted back to a coaster, but not before they fired a salvo when it was announced that hostilities had ceased. It now carried a cargo of coal from Blythe to Fulham, back to Hull for grain for Amsterdam, and then to Emden in Germany to pick up scrap iron from the decommissioned U-boat pens. This was then taken to Grangemouth in Scotland. Finally, after docking in London, Len was released from the merchant fleet pool there. He returned to Borth to marry his sweetheart Betty in 1947. He was a hotelier in Borth from that time until his retirement.

Stephen, Len's son, served in the Royal Navy for twelve years (1964–1976) in radio communications. He served at *HMS Brighton* on *HMS Manxman* and *HMS Devonshire*. Stephen also served on

HMS Malcolm, which was a fisheries protection vessel. During this time two quirky events took place. Once in Gibraltar, as he and shipmates were wending their way down a street, he heard a laugh that he immediately recognized, coming from another group. It was Borth man Peter Rice, a squadron leader in the RAF.

The other occasion was when Frank Davies and family members had gone from Borth on a once in a lifetime trip to see an elderly aunt who had emigrated to West Australia in 1920. Frank had gone to the toilet in a Freemantle hotel where they were having a family reunion dinner and was standing in the urinals next to a tall young matelot who looked at him and said, 'Don't I know you from somewhere?'

The unfazed Frank Davies laconically replied, 'Of course you do, you silly bugger, I have lived next door to you for the last twenty-five years.' They both collapsed with laughter and Frank, over several glasses of ale, explained why he was so far from home. After Stephen left the navy, he moved to the Foreign Office, and remained in the civil service before recently retiring.

William 'Billy' Williams

William Wynne Williams served in the Royal Navy from 1942 to 1946. At the beginning of the Second World War 'Billy Penbont' was unofficially, at sixteen years old, in charge of the Borth home guard group and went on many exercises with them. He was educated at Ardwyn Grammar School where he assisted with the training of the school's army cadets. When he informed the headmaster that he would be joining up immediately he came of age, he was told that an application for a commission in the Royal Welch Fusiliers had already been forwarded. This was no surprise as

Navigator Yeoman Billy Williams, during World War Two

the headmaster was also Colonel of the First Battalion Cardiganshire Home Guard. An argument ensued as Billy was adamant he wanted to join the navy. The well-meaning headmaster thought he was doing his pupil a favour thinking that a man with potential could get a commission quickly in the army, whereas the navy still looked to the public school system for its leaders. Another factor was that for all navy personnel fitness was paramount and only one in fifty got in to the service – after all there were no doctors, surgeons or dentists aboard the smaller ships.

However, Billy persevered and was summoned to appear before an Admiralty Selection Board in Bristol, but was not accepted. After completing his basic training at HMS Raleigh, Torpoint near Plymouth, he was recommended for a commission in the RNVR. He took preliminary training at Portsmouth, followed by the required period of sea service in a Hunt class destroyer. After this he went to HMS King Alfred at Hove for further suitability tests. Billy returned to Portsmouth to successfully complete a pilot's course, then back to HMS King Alfred, where the bulk of the course would be completed at Lancing College, Shoreham-by-Sea; which were premises commandeered by the Royal Navy for the duration of the war. A few days before the commissioning ceremony, he and others were informed that a further period of sea-time was required. This time he did a tour of duty on a minesweeper.

Exasperated, he decided to forgo the frustrating business of gaining a commission and he became a navigator yeoman. He went on to serve on *HMS Stephenson*, a Hunt class destroyer; *HMS Onyx*, a fleet minesweeper and then *HMS Hooke*, a Captain class frigate, whose main role was to sink submarines. He was involved in convoy protection and became embroiled in the battle of the Atlantic. This vessel was part of a group of five plus an escort carrier, which chased down U-boats in a vast area between the Azores and Iceland.

During this time the refuelling station was at Belfast, where they anchored off Bangor for a complete refuelling and replenishing of arms and stores. As he was navigator's yeoman at the time he remembers seeing the sealed orders after one refuelling stop, which stated that their two predecessors had been lost – not a thing to fill one with confidence. It was a very dangerous theatre of operations and as Billy says, 'all thoughts of an official commission were out of the question as the war had moved on apace and I was fully involved in this and comfortable as far as my position went vis a vis a commission'. Toward the end of the war he was involved in the D-day landings. With hostilities over, he spent a year in Australian waters before returning home and demobilizing.

Billy had always dreamed of becoming an architect, but after coming home there was a short period of indecision. The remainder of his working life was to be in the veterinary investigation service of the Ministry of Agriculture, Food and Fisheries, which was also involved with the Ministry of Overseas Development. Billy once went to the Falkland Islands to advise farmers there on sheep breeding. In his retirement he often spends a few months a year at Borth. A kind intelligent person, he provides one of the last links with local events before and during World War Two. He, like so many others, will not divulge the worst aspects of his war time experiences.

David Williams

David, Billy's brother, did his national service in the Royal Navy from June 1947 to August 1949. He spent all his time on aircraft carriers, the *HMS Venerable* that later became *Karel Doorman*, *HMS Implacable* and *HMS Illustrious*. The latter was a flying training vessel, which had distinguished itself in the Second World War at the battle of Toranto. He recalls the incredible quirky nature of it all: traditions that would seem outdated were adhered to as if still in the Nelson era. He was chosen to be the captain's messenger. This 'cushy number', as he calls it, was an eye-opener to all the procedures that the ship's command practiced.

Many sailors doing their national service did not in fact ever leave harbour, so did no sea-time. David remembers meeting up with another naval recruit from Welshpool on the train on his way to join up, and as fate would have it, on David's way home after serving his time he met the same recruit also finishing. As they swapped notes David was astounded to find that the Welshpool man had never ventured out of the Tamar River, where he had spent the entire two years scraping, painting and cocooning redundant warships. Conversely, David's career took him on continual aircraft carrier exercises in the Mediterranean and the mid-Atlantic.

David recalls one occasion when he and the rest of the crew of the *Implacable*, were in Bangor, Northern Ireland, to replace the crew of the *Illustrious*. The general public knew nothing of this. Prior to the changeover David and the rest of the crew had been ashore drinking, and whilst in high spirits they raided a penny arcade and took back on board dozens of various machines. Soon all hell broke loose as word went about that the crew of the *Implacable* were a disgrace etc. etc. Of course, the next day was given over to welcoming the 'new' crew of the *Illustrious*, which unbeknown to the public were recently the rampaging crew of the *Implacable*.

On his return home, being a bit footloose, and still with a measure of wanderlust, he resumed his work as an electrician and he joined Bertram Mills' Circus as they toured the country and wintered in London. After marrying he settled down in Borth and eventually became a leading technician in what was then Ardwyn Grammar School.

David has always been a keen photographer, and in that rôle has recorded many of the villagers and the changing surroundings, amassing a visual record of Borth during the last half century.

The Williams brothers' family's involvement with the sea had a sad aspect as their sister Megan's first husband Robert Jones, a Merchant Navy man, was torpedoed three times in one night, as two rescuing ships were themselves sunk in a matter of hours south of Greenland in a murderous attack by a German U-boat. He was eventually landed in Newfoundland and hospitalised for a long time, but he never really recovered from that experience.

Dolybont Mariners

Dolybont and Penybont are one and the same small village, which has provided a host of mariners as well as some soldiers and airmen. Of its seafarers, there was Captain John Edwards (1812-57) of the schooner *Reform*, who lived at Taicannol. Thomas James (b. 1822) was mate on the 168-ton brig *Squire*; Captain Enoch James (b. 1827) was owner and commander of the schooner *Falcon*; Thomas James (b. 1852), the son of Captain Enoch James, was crewmember and later bosun on the brig *Naomi*. He passed his examination as first mate at Liverpool in October 1873. He had been taught by Lewis Roderick at Borth, and he went on to serve on the sailing vessels *Ethel Ann* and the *Copernicus* and later passed as captain in 1881.

Iorwerth Williams served in the Royal Navy in World War One. He was son of the local stonemason whom the Williams brothers remember as their local barber. Captain David Ellis was master in 1908, survived both World Wars, and retired to Llys Iago in Penybont.

Percy Pearce was in the Royal Navy at the end of the Second World War, and after going on a trip to America, his talk was punctuated with the slang of that country: 'howdy partner', etc. Tragically, he died as a young man when he accidentally fell down an old lead mine shaft. Edward Wood served in the Royal Navy in World War Two as a radar technician; he lived in Dolwen House, and after the war taught at a school for the blind. His sister, Dorothy Wood, served in the WRNS during World War Two, and later became a teacher.

Another Royal Navy World War Two veteran was Glyn Shaw. He was a noted wag, and in a wartime forces football match, recognized Eddie Williams (brother of matelots David and Billy), who served in the RAF in the crowd in front of him. Glyn immediately began shouting 'Come on Dolybont' and 'Come on Carron Jones' to Eddie's amazement and amusement. (Carron Jones was a beloved preacher in the area who lived at Dolybont) Glyn Shaw ended up in Australia, initially as a dog-handler trainer, and later working at a post office in Sydney.

Gareth and Thomas Raw-Rees

Gareth Raw-Rees was the son of First World War army veteran Captain Raw-Rees. The family lived, as some of the descendants still do, at Brynbwl Farm, Borth. At the outbreak of the Second World War, Gareth was a cabin boy on the *King Edwin* voyaging to Murmansk to collect timber for Australia, and thence to South America. However, as war was declared the ship was redirected to London. Gareth was always susceptible to boils as a child, and while at Murmansk developed a severe boil in his ear, which meant he had to be operated on by a Russian doctor. After this he was deaf, and deemed unfit for further service. Eventually he recovered from the operation and never suffered boils again, despite continuing hearing problems. He prospered as an agricultural entrepreneur, and held many important posts, including that of the High Sheriff of Cardiganshire.

Gareth's younger brother, Thomas Kinsey Raw-Rees (1931–2000), went as a purser on the *Oriana* in 1950, commanded by his uncle Captain Roberts of Borth. He went on several voyages to the Antipodes. He returned to farm Brynbwl and contributed to the local community, holding various posts with the County Council.

Richard William Roberts

Tom and Gareth's uncle, Richard William Roberts (1901–1978), went to sea in 1916 following a 200-year maritime family tradition. He was made Lieutenant Commander during the Second World War, and he won the DSC whilst serving on the first *Oronsay* as Commodore of the assault convoy for the invasion of Madagascar. The *Oronsay* was torpedoed off West Africa. For his textbook evacuation of the ship, without loss of life, despite passengers and crew being in lifeboats for nine days, he was awarded an OBE.

Amongst the many posts he held he was elected President of the Mercantile Marine Service Association, the master mariners' organization. He was captain of the *Samkansa* (1944-7), the *Oronsay, Otranto* and the *Orontes* and later staff captain of these vessels. His wife Mary was Tom and Gareth Raw-Rees' auntie, and she and her husband had at one time lived in Fishguard, then moved back to Borth and then retired to live in Llandre at the house appropriately named Oronsay. Captain Roberts was a kindly man and had helped many a Borth lad, such as the Raw-Rees boys, Ivor Williams, Tydu, Hevin Evans of Clarach and David Tink. Another uncle of Gareth and Tom's, William Rees, was an Anglican minister who served as Padre in the Royal Navy in the First World War, and again as Padre in the Second World War, but this time with the RAF.

Ivor Williams Tŷ du was a steward with the Orient Line and voyaged from Europe to Australia on the *Otranto* under the command of Captain Roberts. He had initially set his heart on working on deck, but his eyesight let him down, so his only option was to serve as a steward. Ivor left the sea after a few years to work locally.

Clarach Mariners

Tiny Clarach has provided a few seamen over the years, many a wife for Borth mariners, and even a ship-owner. Captain Evan Williams (b. 1809), at Penybont Cottage, Llangorwen, was mate on the *Pacific* of Monmouth by 1840, and later commanded the local vessel *Aberystwyth* in 1852. A relative of the Captain was master mariner John Williams of Borth, who commanded the barque *Glendovey*, which at 588 tons was the largest sailing ship from Aberdyfi, on which he circumnavigated the globe many times. My great-great-great-grandmother came from Llangorwen in the 1780s. Henry Osborne Smith of Clarach owned one of the last sloops in the area, the 25-ton *Champion*. In 1906, she was run by David Jenkins, an Aberystwyth fisherman, and also his son, another fisherman, Theopholus Jenkins. This sturdy old vessel was broken up in 1917. Hefin Evans (b. 1937) became a steward after training at T. S. Vindicatrix, and his friend, Trevor Williams (b. 1934), of Porth Angel Farm, was an AB. These two friends were like chalk and cheese, Trevor being quiet, calm and reticent, whilst Hefin was ebullient and constantly involved in all manner of escapades.

Hefin's first vessel was the tanker *Stanwell*, travelling back and forth to the Red Sea. Later having missed a ship because of high jinks, he was suspended from the Swansea Pool of seamen, and because of this he was obliged to do national service in the army. He detested army life and exaggerated an arm injury, to the extent that he was discharged. He then went back to sea on the Orient Line for a time under Captain Roberts of Borth. He later sailed on Cape Mail vessels, including the *Stirling Castle* and the *Fontaine Castle*. After leaving the sea, Hefin's perennial anti-authoritarian stance saw him traverse the local landscape and waterways as a poacher, interspersed with building work.

Gwyndaf Evans

Gwyndaf Evans (b. 1938) was the son of railway worker Trevor Evans. Gwyndaf's grandfather was affectionately known as Griff 'Y Crossing Borth', who is commemorated as such on his gravestone. Gwyndaf came from a large family who lived for a number of years at Station House Borth. After leaving school at fifteen, he found himself in Birmingham looking for a job. He hated all the aspects of industrialized post-war cities; they seemed dull and drab, and rationing added to the gloom. After seeing a poster depicting life at sea, he decided to join the Royal Navy. He was to spend eleven years altogether at sea, from 1954 until 1965.

He began his training at HMS Raleigh as a stoker. His first seagoing vessel was *HMS Ocean*, which was involved in the Suez Crisis. After bombarding Port Said, Gwyndaf witnessed the aftermath of conflict, as many of the wounded, including sailors and

Gwyndaf Evans,
grandson of 'Griff y Crossing Borth'

Egyptian civilians, were treated aboard ship. The most unpleasant memory was disposing of limbs in the furnaces. His next vessel was *HMS Drake* and then *HMS Eagle* which was the sister ship of the *HMS Ark Royal*. By this time, he had become a stoker leading hand. His travels took him to South Africa, Australia, the Mediterranean and Scandinavia.

Gwyndaf's next posting was to HMS Goldcrest based in Pembrokeshire. However, in one of his many scrapes he 'borrowed' a police car, and with a few of his shipmates as passengers, drove it back to base. There was a hue and cry so he decided to hide in a laundry basket. In the end it all caught up with him and he was demoted.

By this time he was already married. Upon hearing of the imminent birth of his daughter at Borth, he decided to hitch-hike home, but only got as far as Haverfordwest where he got involved in a brawl helping his shipmates. He got locked up for a time, and only saw his daughter a week later.

As he says, he always got away lightly with these escapades because he was a keen cross-country runner and a very good footballer. He played for the *HMS Eagle* team, and later for the Mediterranean Fleet eleven. By the time he was on *HMS Diamond*, he was leading hand again, and he did a couple of stints on *HMS Defender* and *HMS Duchess*. He returned to serve on *HMS Diamond*, which voyaged to the Mediterranean, the Baltic and went to the small port of Sunsvalt, just north of Stockholm. The captain of the *Diamond* had served with the Mayor of that town, and Gwyndaf remembers the incredible reception they received with bands playing and the whole town out welcoming them.

On HMS Goldcrest he was a great friend of David Jones of Aberystwyth, better known as Dai Cwmparc. They were both in the same football team, and were often flown around for matches in a small plane as far north as Lossiemouth in Scotland.

Long after leaving the Navy, Gwyndaf was invited to return to *HMS Ocean*. His son-in-law, Desmond Enoch, was warrant officer in charge of 800 marines on the new *Ocean*. Gwyndaf and his daughter went on a twenty-four-hour complimentary trip on this vessel to the Channel Islands and back. Gwyndaf was so used to the protocols and disciplines of naval life in the 1950s that he was surprised by being piped up to the bridge and embarrassed when the captain forsook any formality and hugged him, saying, 'Welcome back, my boy'.

He recalls Benidorm in the early 1960s as a sleepy little Spanish town when he visited there on the *HMS Diamond*. The approaches were so shallow that during their ten-day stop-over the crew built a little stone jetty so they could land via the ships' boat; apparently its remains are still there.

Being a sportsman was a great help to Gwyndaf, as often if he fell asleep during lectures or the like, he would have to report to his Commander. When he arrived for the expected disciplinary outcome things inevitably changed when his record was checked, as the next thing he knew was, 'Put the kettle on, Evans'. This would be followed by long discussions about impending football matches or cross-country runs.

Gwyndaf will never forget running a race wearing his Welsh shirt, when a car drew up and out of the passenger window, his then Commander said to him, 'Boy, remember what that shirt is that you are wearing,' and as Gwyndaf says, 'It gave me a huge fillip and I ran like the wind.' He misspent his youth gloriously, courtesy of the Royal Navy. Prospects seemed bleak in the Service when he left, but nowadays, he believes he would have stayed on in the Royal Navy for much longer.

Brian Clare

Brian Clare (b. 1932) lived with his parents and siblings in Glanwern. After leaving Ardwyn Grammar School at the first opportunity, he took whatever jobs were available around Borth. For a time he drove a diesel locomotive carting away the spoil from the Dyfi embankment renovations at Ynyslas. It was bitterly cold in winter and he remembers being tossed a bundle of oily rags during his lunch break, to make a fire with. The sixteen-year-old time reflected on his future; he, like many other local lads, viewed Borth in summer as a joy with new friends to be made, girls to chase; surrounded by an air of excitement and expectation. Unfortunately, this ended abruptly at the end of August, and generations of boys hung around the old bus shelter near Canteen Stores, pondering the looming winter, and their immediate future.

Brian decided it was time to go; he packed a small case, and with twenty-seven shillings in his pocket, caught the train to Liverpool. He had relatives there, and a place to stay. His Aunt Madge, who came to live in Borth later, proved to be invaluable; she organized a meeting for Brian with a representative from Cunard Line. That august company agreed to sponsor him, and off he went to Sea School at Gravesend. He enjoyed his training as a steward, and left with a proficiency award.

On 20 January 1950 he went on his first voyage on the *Samaria* as cabin boy, whose pay was £7 per month. This vessel was a large old-fashioned liner being used to carry 800 displaced persons from Germany to Halifax, Nova Scotia and Quebec. Brian shared, with twelve other crew-members, a cabin situated directly over the propellers. Not only was it noisy, but also, by the second week out, it was quite smelly.

After three transatlantic voyages on this vessel, he joined a cargo ship *Statesman*, an ex-American liberty ship. The accommodation was much better, and the voyage more exotic, visiting seventeen ports in South America and the West Indies, and including a visit to

Galvaston and up river to Houston, Texas. This was a memorable three-month trip.

Brian's next vessel was the *Petrel*, a small coaster that occasionally took five days to sail from Southampton to London. Often she would proceed only after favourable weather forecasts, and it was on one of these in-between-foul-conditions dashes across the English Channel that he was seasick for the first time.

After promotion to assistant steward, he went on the *Athlone Castle*, a two-class passenger liner (first and tourist), to South Africa. From there he joined the *Tudor Prince*, a cargo vessel sailing from Swansea to several Mediterranean ports. Brian's next trip on the *Nicoya*, a Fyffes banana boat, was quite unpleasant: they went to West Africa where it was unbearably hot and plagued by mosquitoes, it took quite a while to load the cargo: 97,000 stems of bananas. Luckily, the next Fyffes ship, the *Gahlito*, went to Central America and the West Indies, an area Brian loved and visited often. Although a cargo vessel, she carried a hundred passengers.

Brian's next vessel, the 25,600-ton liner *Andes*, was the largest he had been on, and the last of his seafaring career. This vessel sailed from Southampton to ports in Brazil and Argentina. Again promoted, he was now earning the princely sum of £27 a month.

By then he had spent nearly six years at sea, which he described as the happiest and most adventurous and carefree period in his life. He recalls with amusement how one summer, at home on leave, he was inveigled by Doug Fleet, the manager of the Grand Hotel, Borth, to do a stint at his restaurant, where he was promoted as a Cunard Line steward, which was a great malarkey as all he really did was parade about in his uniform.

He found to his surprise that despite his sea-time he would still have to do his national service. This proved a dilemma, as Brian was not prepared to go back down the ranks, as it were. The only other option, apart from escaping the country, was to become a coalminer. As he had kept contact with many Borth summer holiday acquaintances that lived in the Midlands, it was there that he joined the National Coal Board and worked as a coalminer for another five years. At twenty-seven years old, he decided to go into business selling and maintaining sewing machines. This business expanded and there was even a Clare sewing machine on the market. During this time, he married and started a family, and when this initial business declined with the advent of cheap imported clothing, he converted his various shops into art galleries and suppliers. He is now retired and living in Staffordshire, but his fond memories of his childhood and youth in Borth still burn bright.

David Tink

In 1941, David Tink (b. 1938) and his brother John were sent to live with their widowed grandmother Gertrude Hannah Whiterod, at West End, Borth. As David said, 'If it hadn't been for Hitler I would not have been a Borth boy'! David was educated at Upper Borth Primary School under the benevolent dictatorship of Mr James the headmaster, then Ardwyn Grammar School and later HMS Conway Merchant Navy Cadet School on the Menai Strait.

David had become increasingly interested in the sea, partly from reading and listening to his godmother Muriel Kind's stories of her naval experiences. David then joined the Sea Cadet Corps in Aberystwyth and learnt to sail and pull cutters and whalers. Visits to warships paying courtesy visits to Aberystwyth also fuelled his interest in ships. He remembers visiting the battleships *Duke of York* and *Anson*, the destroyers *Wizard, Diamond* and *Relentless*, the frigate *Fleetwood* and the American destroyer *Zellars*. In 1953, just before his fifteenth birthday, he passed the entrance exam to the Conway. In addition to standard school subjects, cadets were taught navigation, chart work, seamanship, signals, ship construction and engineering.

After a while at Conway, David was promoted to junior cadet captain (boats), and as far as he was concerned it was idyllic! From Conway, David secured a cadetship with Blue Star Line. Many of their vessels were refrigerated, bringing home beef from South America; lamb, wool and butter from Australia and New Zealand; grain, timber and fruit from the USA and Canada. Outbound general cargoes consisted of anything from toilet bowls to Rolls Royce cars! Depending upon the size of the vessel and number of crew a cadet's duties were several. In port, one cadet kept the gangway watch from 0700 to 1900 while the others kept a cargo-loading log or ran errands for the chief officer. Entering and leaving ports the senior cadet would be on the bridge keeping the engine movement and helm orders log, answering and relaying messages, and escorting the pilot to and from the pilot ladder. The other cadets would accompany the chief officer forward or the second mate aft while berthing or anchoring.

At sea in coastal waters, watches were maintained on the bridge with the second, third and fourth mates; once 'deep sea', cadets became labourers. Under the supervision of the bosun they chipped rust, washed and painted bulkheads, cleaned bilges and polished brass! Cadets also maintained the lifeboats – painting interiors, greasing rigging, oiling davits and replenishing stores, fresh water and emergency flares. With the ship's carpenter they swept empty holds and laid dunnage in preparation for cargo, and steered the ship and kept lookout, as well as cleaning their own cabins and washing and ironing their own clothes.

David's first ship was the 12,790-ton *Brisbane Star* built by Cammell Laird in 1936: a veteran of Malta convoys, having taken part in Operation Pedestal. Despite having her bows blown off in a torpedo attack which reduced her speed to 3 knots, she was one of only five merchant vessels to arrive in Malta, out of fourteen.

In January 1956 David sailed from London to Hamburg and back to London, where they discharged the previous voyage's cargo in Avonmouth and then sailed for Australia with a refuelling stop in Tenerife. In Melbourne he met an old friend from the Conway and after a couple of beers went ice-skating. He swiftly learnt that one should not chase blondes around an ice rink unless one can skate properly. A broken kneecap resulted in hospitalisation in Melbourne and the *Brisbane Star* sailed home without her most junior cadet!

David came home on the *Otranto* solely due to 'the old girls and old boys network'! His mother chatted to her next-door neighbour Mrs Roberts in Sea Haven, wife of Captain R. Roberts DSC, RD, RNR, who was in command of the *Otranto* on the Australia run. Captain Roberts duly chatted to an old friend (Blue Star Line's marine superintendent in Sydney) and so David found himself homeward bound on the *Otranto*, one of the Orient Line's large two funnelled, pre-war passenger liners. To complete the Borth triumvirate, David's cousin Ivor Williams of Tŷ du happened to be a crewmember. Spoilt by the passengers (as a seventeen-year-old on crutches), and by the crew (as he was officially classed as a Distressed British Seaman), he had a very enjoyable voyage home via Suez. Invariably Captain Roberts invited him to the bridge during entering and leaving harbour so he could continue to learn the duties of a ship's officer.

After a long recuperation, David eventually returned to sea in November when he joined the *Seattle Star* in Liverpool. This old ship had a very cranky steering with a rudder indicator that had no relationship to the rudder's position. So until one was used to it, the ship tended to wander over the ocean. The mate would stand in the wheelhouse alternately praying and cursing – praying that David would get it right and cursing when the rapid clicking of the gyro compass told him that he was getting it wrong! On the homeward voyage in a North Atlantic hurricane, the steering packed up in the middle of the night; emergency steering was rigged but before it was engaged, the ship broached, the deck cargo of timber shifted and heavy seas smashed a lifeboat and flooded the ship's galley. They lived off corned beef sandwiches and cocoa for the next three days!

There was a falling out with the master, which was all to do with a radio that David owned which was capable of picking up UK broadcasts in the South Atlantic. The Old Man, a cricket fanatic, was unable to pick up the test matches on his set. He was furious that David preferred to listen to Radio Luxemburg and didn't report the cricket scores to him daily!

During leave in July 1958, a Blue-Star-Line-franked letter addressed to Mr D. A. Tink (and not to Cadet D. A. Tink) arrived at his home. It requested Mr. D. A. Tink to take up the position of 4 Officer aboard the *Sydney Star*, which he was to join in Liverpool on Friday 25 July, at a salary of £28 per month. For his first watch, just after sailing from Liverpool, the chief officer was on the bridge as the ship headed west from the Bar Light Vessel, rounding the Skerries, and heading south through Cardigan Bay. Next morning the master and chief officer came on the bridge at 0800, conferred briefly, then the Chief Officer said to David, 'You're on your own,' and he and Captain Pitcher disappeared! This was possibly one of the most thrilling moments of David's time at sea. It was four months before the mate joined him on the bridge again: that was at the end of a round the world voyage and they were steaming slowly through the Straits of Dover in poor visibility!

After a short stint on the *English Star*, David's next ship was the *Rhodesia Star*, which he joined in Hull. She was of all-metal

David Tink – a varied career: from delivering Rolls Royce cars to flying helicopters

construction – tables, doors, bunks, cupboards all rattled noisily once the engines were turning. None of Blue Star ships were fitted with radar. However, it was necessary to have a radar observer's certificate before sitting for second mate's certificate. The company sent its cadets to the Sir John Cass Nautical College in London to obtain the radar qualification. David and fellow cadets steamed up and down the Thames in their training vessel for a fortnight learning the theory and practice before sitting the exam. On his next vessel, the *Californian Star*, he prepared himself to sit for the Board of Trade second mate's certificate.

David was becoming enamoured with the idea of flying – but also wanted to stay at sea, so the obvious next choice was the Fleet Air Arm. However, if he applied for fixed-wing then it was likely, with his navigational background, he would be streamlined as an observer (navigator). By 1959 the Royal Navy had started offering short service commissions as helicopter pilots, and David duly applied. After basic naval training on *HMS Thunderer* and *HMS Seahawk* he was awarded his 'wings' and sent to *HMS Osprey* (RNAS Portland) in Dorset for advanced and operational training.

After David retired from the Royal Navy he became a civilian pilot for the North Sea oil industry. Apart from the routine of oil support operations and training (both aircraft and simulator) the job of chief training captain took him abroad fairly often with trips to the Falkland Islands, Malaysia, Ireland, Norway, and Dubai.

John Cory

John Cory (b. 1952) was educated at Dinas Secondary School. His mother came from a family of mariners from Llanon, and she served in the Wrens during the Second World War. At fifteen, having become interested in a seafaring career, he joined the Royal Navy. He initially signed on for nine years and did his training on HMS Ganges. His first seagoing voyage was on the frigate *HMS Euryalus*, going to the Far East and Australia. John's interest lay in communications. He was for a time shore-based in Dorset at HMS Osprey, and became involved in what is known as the Electronic Warfare Segment – this was still in the time of the Cold War.

His next vessels were the *HMS Leander* and *HMS Tenby*. The latter vessel was essentially an officers' training ship. In between trips, John attended college at Dartmouth to hone his skills in the field of communications. The result was that he became a leading hand within a few years. He was then recommended as a potential petty officer. This was against his own better judgment as he felt that he needed more experience in the man-management side. However, he went for the examinations and passed, specializing in electronic warfare. There was a shortage of officers in his field at the time, and so at the age of twenty-one, his promotion came through whilst he was at sea, and he was told by the captain to change mess decks. Even his rank insignia had been forwarded to the *HMS Charybis*.

John was then sent to HMS Raleigh, which was a shore-based teaching establishment dealing with new naval entrants. As he wryly recalls, before he could teach them sailing, he himself had to have a crash course in that particular skill. He taught a lot of classes of young recruits who had only just joined up. In a twenty-five year career, he considers this to have been the most satisfying period. At twenty-four years old, he joined his first ship *HMS Phoebe* as Petty Officer in charge of his own electronic warfare department. This vessel was involved in a six-week 'work-up' off Portland; its purpose was to test the crew as a working team in given conditions. After due consideration, the Admiral of the Fleet gives a vessel the seal of approval.

John's team did not do well; consequently he was demoted to leading hand, which proved that his initial doubts about his premature promotion were well founded. He then joined HMS *Devonshire*, a guided missile destroyer, and spent a year escorting HMS *Ark Royal* on her final voyage showing the flag in American ports. John's next vessel HMS *Naiad*, sailed to South America, where again he was recommended for petty officer. This time he confidently accepted, as he now felt more self-assured and experienced. He had in the meantime made sure that as he was in electronic communications, logistics and ship recognition, that he should learn some of the older skills such as Morse code and semaphore.

Around this time he married Sian, and they were living at Dolybont. He did another Portland 'work-up' on HMS *Bacchante* and this time passed with flying colours, primarily as he says, because it had a good crew. He was posted to the Persian Gulf during the Iran/Iraq war, where the Royal Navy were playing the role of observers; showing the flag and protecting merchant shipping in the Straits of Hormuz.

In 1982 John did a six-month shore stint on HMS Drake, looking after accommodations of all things; it was essentially a recreational posting. John would often come home to Dolybont during these shore-based postings. He met Stephen Brown of Borth, through the chalkboard messages that naval personnel left offering lifts all over the country. From that time Stephen provided John with regular transport back home on many week-ends.

John's next vessel was HMS *Brazen*, which was a newly-built vessel with up-to-date equipment, so he went on a refresher course to cope with the latest technology. This was at the time of the Falklands War, and soon he found himself on HMS *Brilliant*, which had returned from the Falklands campaign. With a new crew, they returned to the Falklands. It was a very edgy time, and the vessel was well prepared, in case of a renewed Argentinean attack, that the whole crew was instructed to write last letters home.

After returning from South Georgia, he returned to the shore based HMS Osprey. During this time he received the news that he had been promoted to chief petty officer. In that capacity he joined the *HMS Argonaut,* which should have been scrapped after the Falklands, but it spent the next eighteen months on patrol in the North Atlantic. John finally left the *Argonaut* after twenty-five years service.

Edward 'Teddy' Davies

Edward 'Teddy' Davies (b. 1941) joined the Merchant Navy in 1957. He had left school at fifteen and worked with Johnnie Thomas, an ex-seaman, until he was old enough to join up. He went to the National Sea Training School at Sharpness and whilst there won a boxing medal. He joined the Swansea pool and got a berth on the BP oil tanker *El Moro*, which took him on a five-month trip calling in at Kuwait, Durban, ports in Argentina and Venezuela and even rounding Cape Horn. He went on the *El Moro* twice, and by sheer coincidence briefly met up with another Borth man, radio operator Gethin Evans in the Suez Canal. It was very much a hello and goodbye situation, as Gethin was on an Esso tanker going the other way. Teddy later joined the Cardiff Pool and was on coasters for the Greenfield Line for a few voyages, which hardly varied. They went from Cardiff to Durham then to Cornwall for china clay for Preston; after this back to Cardiff for coal slag for St Malo in France and back to Cardiff again. After four years Teddy caught a very severe ear infection that precluded any further service. Since returning home, he has run a painting and decorating partnership with his brother Glyn.

Michael Edwards

Michael Edwards (b. 1948) joined the Merchant Navy at seventeen years old, and did his training at T. S. Vindicatrix. He went to see Dr. Lloyd Davies for his medical, and the next day jumped on a train to go to the training camp. He learned boat-handling, rope work, cargo dynamics and basic navigation. After ten weeks, he passed his examination, and as he says, 'It was surprising how many fell by the wayside because they simply seemed unable to tie a knot'. During this time, a great camaraderie existed within his group of recruits, but sadly he never saw any of them ever again.

Having signed on to the Cardiff Pool, he made a quick trip home before joining his first ship, a small coaster that traded between Bristol and Liverpool. He returned to Borth from Liverpool and ten days later, he joined the 70,000-ton tanker *British Bombadier*, which sailed out of Milford. He voyaged through the Mediterranean and entered the Suez Canal. He had never felt as hot as he did in Kuwait, especially as they tied up alongside a mammoth Japanese tanker, where the radiated heat of its metal hull increased the general discomfort of those working on the *British Bombadier*. Mike and his mates went on a tour of the Japanese giant, whose crew constantly asked them for whisky.

From there, they sailed to Venezuela where they tied up to an offshore submarine pipeline terminal. Whilst they were taking oil on board, they heard heavy gunfire from the shore, presumably some kind of revolution. As Mike says he did not know what was going on, but the captain decided to sail away immediately, in case they got hit.

The moorings were slipped a bit too rapidly as the oil pipe was disengaged, consequently spilling a huge amount of oil into the sea, and all over the decks, which took over a fortnight to clean up. During this speedy departure, the ship was obviously moving before the bow mooring line was detached. Then Mike heard the ominous noise of a 'singing line'. The older hands immediately screamed, 'Dive for cover!' and Mike and others flung themselves under the nearest winch. The snapped line was singing as it whiplashed through all the standing bollards and vents, like a knife cutting through cheese. The tanker arrived back at Tilbury only half loaded with oil, and they spent the return voyage cleaning the oil and repairing the damage caused by the mooring line accident.

After a brief visit to Borth, Mike joined another, somewhat smaller, tanker, the *Regent Caribou*. They left Liverpool for Copenhagen on Christmas Eve, with the crew much the worse for drink. They had not been there a day when a vast contingent of police boarded the vessel, searching not for contraband and the like, but the missing head of the famous mermaid statue in the harbour. (It was found years later and reset on the plinth, the culprits having been students.) After leaving Denmark, they crossed the Atlantic and headed up the Amazon to the port of Manaus, a town miles up the river that boasted an opera house, Teatro Amazonas, where Enrico Caruso had sung.

Before they reached Manaus, as the ship was slowly sailing against the fierce river current, an accident happened that was deeply disturbing for all the crew. As the ship was progressing, dozens of canoes, with the local natives on board, drew alongside, and the crew threw them tins of beans and apples and other fruit in a gesture of friendship. For some inexplicable reason, one of the galley boys decided to go down and get a closer view of the canoes, even boarding one, and in doing so slipped and fell into the river, never to be seen again. The lifeboats were launched and the ship was anchored, and even the natives in the canoes were searching frantically for the young crew member, but to no avail. The ship's boats were swept downstream and it took a couple of days for everyone to return. Instead of the long-awaited revelry ashore at Manaus, a terrible gloom settled over the ship.

When Mike's ship returned to Liverpool, everyone's name was taken, in case they were called to the enquiry that was being set up to investigate the galley boy's death. As Michael states, 'Thankfully I was not called.' Strangely, the vessel itself was soon scrapped. This incident sullied things a bit for Michael, and he did not return to sea for a month or two. He next took a short trip on a coaster, and a couple of months later, he was ashore as his father had been taken ill, and died soon afterwards. After five years at sea, Michael decided to join the army, which he had wanted to do for a long time. He was six years in the army, doing three stints in Northern Ireland. After leaving the army, Michael and his wife Shirley went to live in Anglesey, where he has run a successful building business with his son.

Mike Birch

Mike Birch's great grandfather, on his mother Nancy's side, was Ferdinand Honey, who in partnership with Alfred Reed, began the Prowse Line of Birkenhead. They started with sailing ships but gradually moved to steamers: according to Nancy Birch, this was why Ferdinand Honey withdrew from the partnership, which later became Coast Lines. Her father George Honey was employed as marine traffic officer with Coast Lines for nearly fifty years. Mike himself started his maritime career by attending HMS Conway, the merchant navy training school at Anglesey. He spent three and a half years there learning shipboard duties, navigation, seamanship, ship construction, ship- and-boat handling and meteorology.

At the age of eighteen Mike passed out to join his first shipping company, British and Commonwealth, an amalgamation of several shipping companies, the major ones being Clan Line and Union Castle. He was with them for seven years sailing as cadet on the *Clan Malcolm*, fourth officer on the passenger ship *Windsor Castle* and third officer on a variety of cargo ships including the *Clan Maciver*. He was also on the tanker *Hector Heron*, mainly between the ports of South Africa and UK.

The passenger ships, more commonly referred to as 'mail boats', carried surface mail between Southampton and Capetown. They ran on a very strict timetable, leaving Southampton with the last line letting go at precisely 1600 hours on Thursday arriving at the Capetown pilot station at 0600 nine days later, on the dot! The first mail boat he sailed on was the flag ship of the fleet the *Windsor Castle*, 2000 passengers in two classes with 900 crew-members. He also went on a few voyages on the smaller mail boat, the *Southampton Castle*, on the same run but southbound, going via Ascension Island to pick up deck passengers to take to St Helena before going onto Capetown. These passengers were St Helenians, who worked on Ascension for periods up to three months.

The Clan Line cargo ships traded between the UK and South

Africa, East Africa or India, and visited some fascinating places. South African ports were comfortable and modern ports, but the same could not be said for most of the East African ports such as Dar es Salaam, Nacala or Tanga. Those were the places that Mike wouldn't choose to return to on holiday. The places that he would go back to are Mombasa, Mauritius and Zanzibar. Zanzibar was a fascinating place. The streets smelt strongly of cloves, huge reinforced wooden doors opened into bars, hotel foyers and private houses. The hotel bars, with their slow ceiling fans circulating the humid air in the dim light evoked images of Humphrey Bogart drinking cocktails.

During Mike's time with British and Commonwealth he got his second mate's ticket and then was employed by Maersk Offshore. He joined the first ship in Esberge, Denmark as mate. They supplied rigs off the Danish coast, plying back and forth in all weathers from violent North Sea storms to dense fog and frozen sea. The work rotas were five weeks on, five weeks off. The company built bigger ships which worked from other North Sea ports in Scotland, so Mike was moved to work out of Peterhead or Aberdeen. After five years with Maersk, Mike got his master's ticket and the company gave him his first command.

Mike had served ten years with Maersk when he saw an advert for a vacancy in pilotage in Portsmouth. Working ashore, and not having to endure the North Sea storms, were good reasons for applying for the post. This was a time when the pilotage regulations were changing and the organisation of pilotage in the Solent was being split into individual ports. Mike was accepted for the position at Portsmouth, essentially a Royal Navy port with most ships being piloted by RN pilots. Mike was one of four commercial ship pilots responsible for the movement of a regular flow of refrigerated cargo ships and the cross channel ferries. This was no mean feat as Mike had to constantly manoeuvre vessels in his charge around moving warships.

Mike left Portsmouth after ten happy years to take up the position of harbour-master at the freshly privatised port of Portland in Dorset. After an armed forces review the Royal Navy decided to dispose of Portland. It was bought by a private company and Mike had the privilege of being the first commercial harbour master. The post required that he set up a marine department and pilotage service. It was 'in at the deep end' though: he took over on January 1st when three ships were in the port and a very strong westerly storm was blowing across the harbour. He got no sleep on his first night! After two years he moved on to marine consultancy for a while, before emigrating to New Zealand. Captain Mike Birch is now Marine Pilot at New Plymouth on the west coast of New Zealand: North Island, under the shadow of the Egmont volcano.

Peter Norrington-Davies

Peter Norrington-Davies was born in 1950 and lived at Dolybont; he was one of three brothers, two of whom joined the army. He was educated at Ardwyn Grammar School, Aberystwyth, and then joined the Royal Navy in 1969 as a cadet at the Britannia Royal Naval College Dartmouth, Class 204. There followed an intense period of basic training when he travelled to the Baltic in the summer. He was at sea on *HMS Torquay* as part of a group of forty cadets who worked and lived as ordinary seamen, doing all the mundane tasks – chipping, painting and general deck duties – and even slept in hammocks.

His second year was spent at sea as a midshipman on *HMS Arethusa*, which was a Leander class frigate. During this time they were patrolling the east coast of Africa and blockading the port of Beira during the Unilateral Declaration of Independence by Rhodesia. He left the area, calling in at the Seychelles and then on to Singapore. Peter was then flown back to Dartmouth to begin his third year, which was primarily academic, including studies in engineering, physics, maths, navigation and languages. He chose to study Norwegian and became competent in this language. This choice was influenced by a memorable hitch-hiking holiday he spent in Norway in the company of Michael Griffiths of Borth and Idwal Steadman of Llangwyrfon. Peter chose to specialize in navigation as he had easily passed his higher mathematics examination, and successfully concluded his third year. He recalls with gratitude the latitude given to him by the naval authorities during this time, as he took up recreational flying to gain his private pilot's licence.

He was lucky enough to be invited by a naval pilot to take a flight in a Hunter jet. The Navy gave him permission to do this as it would broaden his experience. After discussing the flight plan, he phoned his parents at Dolybont to inform them that he would be visiting the area. It was a wonderful experience and when they reached the Dyfi Estuary, they turned south over Cors Fochno and up over the slopes flying over Dolybont where his parents and friends were enthusiastically awaiting his arrival. Then he flew down the valley to Borth, and then south along the coast and inland over Aberystwyth to his old school where his brother Patrick, proudly announced to his school chums, 'That's my brother flying overhead.'

His fourth year courses included communications, gunnery, navigation and mine clearance. This was to broaden his knowledge of the whole gamut of naval operations. During this time, he applied for leave to crew and navigate a large privately-owned cruising vessel, the *Dematra*, which was being taken to Greece for a shipping magnate. He was given naval blessing as it was again deemed appropriate experience.

Whilst doing a communications course at HMS Mercury, he and others found recruitment circulars for submarine duty in their pigeon-holes. To a man, they crumpled the notes up and threw them away. This was a very bad move: if they had read the circular properly they would have noticed that it was to be signed and returned if they did *not* want a post on submarines. Soon afterwards, Peter received notice that he was appointed as a submariner, which threw him into a total panic. He was so desperate that he used a social connection and managed to get an audience with the Second Sea Lord, Sir Gordon Tait, to plead his case. It was all to no avail: even though he pleaded claustrophobia, he was gently persuaded to accept, somewhat reluctantly, that because of his mishandling of the original note, he was now committed. His case was not helped in that at the time there was a shortfall of officers in the submarine division of the navy.

He joined the submarine *HMS Andrew* at Oslo, where he amazed those there with his ability to speak a little Norwegian. He served for a time as a gunnery officer, as this submarine was the last to have a gun deck, but the *Andrew*'s days were over and she was decommissioned in 1974. Peter was then appointed navigation officer on *HMS Orpheus*, an Oberon Class submarine. He was then on *HMS Repulse*, *HMS Conqueror* and then as First Lieutenant of the *Osiris*. He was selected for the Commanding Officer Course on *HMS Perisher* in 1984, and was then given command of *HMS Walrus*. At thirty-two years old, he was now solely responsible for the varied and complex aspects of operating a sophisticated £60,000,000 warship.

Peter was subsequently appointed as a Submarine Operations Officer to Flag Officer Submarines, based at the joint headquarters at Northwood. As he jokingly observes, seven years of his twenty-year service in the Royal Navy were spent under water.

Stephen Richard Brown

Stephen Richard Brown (b. 1957) had wanted to go to sea for as long as he could remember. This is no surprise as his father was from an Aberystwyth seafaring family. His grandfather, Arthur Brown (b. 1898), had gone to sea at eleven years old. Five years later he was badly burnt in an oil fire after being torpedoed in the English Channel. Although he had skin grafts, they were perennially troublesome as the technique was fairly primitive at the time. Arthur wore a silk scarf to hide the scars around his throat and lower face: many mistook this for an affectation. He was a coastguard in Aberystwyth for many years.

Another antecedent, John Robinson Brown (b. 1867), passed as master in 1896 and in 1917 commanded the *SS Cliftonian*. Stephen's antecedents on his mother's side were the Hughes family of mariners. Captain Thomas Hughes commanded the *Picton Castle*, which gave its name to the house they lived in at Upper Borth, and which later became known as the shop Castle Stores.

At sixteen years old Stephen joined the Royal Navy and did his basic training on HMS Ganges. He then joined HMS Collingwood to train as an electrical mechanic. His first seagoing vessel was *HMS Fearless*, a landing craft ship that took marines on exercises. He went to the West Indies and South America visiting Caracas, Cartagena, Barbados and the Virgin Islands. His work included stints in the engine rooms, boats and batteries, boiler rooms, domestic refrigeration, hydraulics and weapons.

His next vessel was *HMS Hecla*, a much smaller vessel that served as a survey ship off the coast of Scotland. This was the one activity that the navy could commercialize: the charts from its surveys were sold to the general public. Stephen served two years altogether on the *Hecla*.

His next posting was the shore-based gunnery school, HMS Cambridge, where he was part of the maintenance crew. He travelled back to Borth on as many weekends as he could. For a time he was the only electrician on board *HMS Argonaut*, voyaging to the Mediterranean. He next went to do a leading weapons electrical course at HMS Collingwood and passed after six months. As he explains, despite not intending to leave the navy, he would sign up for courses to prepare him for civilian life. He did a heavy goods vehicle course, then a refrigeration course, and then promptly signed up for the navy again. When Stephen eventually left the Navy, he worked for an alarm installation company.

One weekend in the early 1980s, he decided to sneak off to Borth on a Thursday afternoon, instead of the Friday, from his fleet maintenance shore base *HMS Defiant*. Unbeknown to him, the hierarchy were trying to find him, as a ship bound for the Falklands urgently required someone with close-range weapons expertise. After a heavy partying weekend in Borth, he arrived back on a Monday, summoned to an office, and given the alternative to either join the vessel *Rangatira*, or face severe punishment for going awol on the previous Thursday. Stephen took the easy option and went to the Falklands.

The *Rangatira* was originally a New Zealand ferry, a floating hotel for oil workers off Scotland, and after that was laid up in Falmouth and fitted out with passenger bunks for RAF and Royal Engineers bound for the Falklands. Oerlikon anti-aircraft guns were installed. Officially, it was Naval party 2070, with fifty-five Royal Navy men on board and a merchant navy crew running the vessel, which carried a thousand passengers. As the Royal Navy complement was first on board, they commandeered the Sporting Man's Bar, which was a leftover from its floating hotel days. The doors were sealed off and a sign was painted on their outside, 'Navy Party 2070 Only, no Others Admitted'. The troops were on a ration of two cans of beer a day; Stephen his and shipmates' 'ration' was bottomless.

They stopped at Ascension Island to refuel, and rumours spread that the vessel was going to become a floating POW ship in Port Stanley. Approaching Port Stanley at around midnight, the ship suddenly struck something and keeled over. The steering was lost and she kept going round and round in a circle, which was dangerous as they were near, or in, a minefield, and it could have been blown up at any minute. Stephen found out later that this fault in the steering had been the cause of her sister ferry being wrecked in New Zealand. Thankfully, they arrived safely and tied up to a buoy at Port Stanley, where they remained for five months just after hostilities ceased.

During this time Steve was also involved with a salvage team repairing an Argentinian gunboat that had been sunk. With the war over most of his time was spent not only on maintenance, but on sentry duty, not so much to watch for the enemy but to ensure that returning troops were not too drunk to negotiate the stern doors.

Stephen's next vessel was the ex-ferry *Norland*, which promptly broke down, so he was shifted to the ex-British Car Rail Ferry *St Edmund*. No sooner had he arrived back in Southampton, than he was flown back to Port Stanley to join *HMS Liverpool*, which in turn soon headed for home and ended up for eight weeks off Murmansk observing Russian ship manoeuvres.

Stephen's next posting was to *HMS Berwick*, and again he ended up patrolling the waters around the Falklands. His last was *HMS Cornwall*, where as Stephen says, it was a year-long cruise to the Arctic Circle, Norway, the Mediterranean, North America and the West Indies. After nearly twenty-one years, he left the Navy.

This book covers the history of only about a third of Borth mariners. From my own childhood, I remember Richard Jenkins, who lived at Gable End. He left Borth in 1956, and all that is known is that he had a successful career in the Royal Navy. A few others have also been omitted because of lack of information, such as Michael Rodaway, Robin Evans, John Gimlett and Dorothy Lathwood. John Williams of Brynllys Farm, whose antecedents on his father's side were sea captains from North Wales, attended HMS Conway training school, but although he passed out, he almost immediately took up a career in agriculture.

I have had to revise the list of master mariners from Borth during the course of recent research, and bring it up to date. In *Welsh Mariners Index*, the Borth listings indicate that the village produced just over 200 captains. The author states it is not a definitive list: some names are missing, such as Captain John Hughes Oddy, Captain John Emlyn Herbert, Captain Edward Lloyd, Captain Norrington-Davies and Captain Mike Birch. One has to include master mariners sailing long before official lists began, and according to the Aberystwyth shipping records, there are a score or more Borth masters such as John Jones, John Rees, Hugh Humphreys, Rhys Lewis and Thomas Thomas, which makes a final tally of approximately

David Hughes,
known as 'Dafydd y Friendship':
the Borth inn's landlord in the late
nineteenth century

230. This is a remarkable figure given the size of the village, and one would not credit this fact by just driving through Borth today. I hope this book has gone some of the way to further flesh out the village's remarkable maritime history.

Companion volume, by the same author

Borth's sea history and folklore
Price: £8
www.carreg-gwalch.com